BUILD
A KICKA$$
SALES TEAM:

Practical Sales Tactics

BY DR. EVE KEDAR

Edited by Colleen Kern

Published by: GWN Publishing
www.GWNPublishing.com

Cover Design: Kristina Conatser

ISBN: 978-1-965971-05-5

TABLE OF CONTENTS

INTRODUCTION

Empowering Sales through Strategic Enablement

The role of sales enablement has never been more critical than in today's rapidly evolving business landscape. Organizations are grappling with informed buyers, complex markets, and the relentless pace of technological innovation. Amid the various challenges, one thing remains constant: Sales teams need to be more agile, knowledgeable, and equipped than ever before.

But how do organizations make this happen?

This book is crafted to effectively address this question and is the result of over 15 years of extensive involvement in the domains of sales enablement, learning and development, and customer education. It serves as a comprehensive guide for sales leaders, enablement professionals, and you if you are passionate about transforming your sales teams into high-impact performers.

Drawing from extensive experience and deep understanding of sales enablement, Dr. Eve Kedar's perspective presents a distinctive approach that effectively merges strategic planning and practical implementation. Her work is grounded in real-world accomplishments, including:

- **Implementing Scalable Onboarding and Certification Programs:** Driving measurable outcomes and fostering community engagement across global organizations.

- **Integrating Generative AI into Learning and Development:** Pioneering the use of AI tools to create best in class training academies and customer education initiatives.

- **Leading Transformational Change:** Managing large-scale training programs that transform complex concepts into easily digestible material, resulting in significant sales growth and team empowerment.

WHO SHOULD READ THIS BOOK

- Sales Leaders looking to drive team performance and align sales strategies with business objectives.

- Sales Enablement Professionals seeking practical tactics and frameworks to enhance their programs.

- Learning and Development Practitioners who are interested in integrating innovative technologies and methodologies into their training initiatives.

- Business Executives and Entrepreneurs aiming to understand how sales enablement can be a strategic lever for growth.

A JOURNEY TOWARD SALES EXCELLENCE

In the pages that follow, you'll embark on a journey that demystifies sales enablement, breaking it down into digestible chapters that each tackle a critical aspect of building high-impact sales teams. From crafting a strategic vision to scaling programs across your organization, this book provides the tools and knowledge necessary to transform your sales enablement efforts.

This book is designed to be a comprehensive roadmap for anyone looking to elevate their sales enablement efforts. Here's what we'll cover:

- **Actionable Frameworks:** Step-by-step guides and models with acronyms like ADDIE, SAM, SEID, EMPOWER, and SCALE that you can implement in your organization.

- **Real-World Examples:** Case studies from industry-leading companies that demonstrate successful sales enablement strategies in action.

- **Practical Tools:** Recommendations for building a robust tech stack, including summaries of essential tools, FAQs, and platforms that enhance sales performance.

- **Expert Insights:** In-depth discussions on integrating emerging technologies like AI, fostering team engagement, and measuring the impact of your initiatives.

- **Continued Learning Resources:** A glossary of key terms, top podcast and book recommendations, and access to additional materials to further your understanding.

Are you ready to elevate your sales organization to new heights?

Let's begin this journey together, leveraging proven tactics, embracing innovation, and ultimately, driving remarkable business results.

Excited to help you build kicka$$ programs with engaging brand exploding communities at ekconsulting.io

Dr. Eve Kedar
Morgan Hill, California
info@Ekconsulting.io
LinkedIn: linkedin.com/in/evekedar

HOW TO USE THIS BOOK

To maximize the benefits of this book:

- **Actively Engage:** At the end of each chapter, you'll find calls to action, a summary and FAQs. Take the time to reflect, engage and connect these learnings to your context.

- **Leverage the Resources:** Utilize the glossary, the FAQs, the tech stack summaries, and podcast recommendations to deepen your understanding and stay updated with industry trends.

- **Join the Conversation:** Connect with peers and professionals in the field. Consider joining online communities to share insights and learn from others and potentially contribute your point of view. Reach out to the author on LinkedIn to join her online community!

Sales enablement is a journey of learning, adaptation, iteration and growth. As you delve into the chapters ahead, remember that the strategies and tactics discussed are starting points to be adjusted, aligned, and adapted for your unique organizational context.

Let's embark on this journey toward building high-impact sales teams and achieving amazingly powerful sales success.

CHAPTER 1

THE CRITICAL ROLE OF SALES ENABLEMENT IN TODAY'S BUSINESS LANDSCAPE

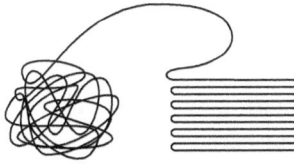

I n an era where buyers are more informed than ever, and markets evolve at lightning speed, sales teams face immense pressure to deliver results. The modern customer conducts extensive research before ever engaging with a salesperson, and with an abundance of options available, loyalty is harder to earn and maintain. Amid this complexity, one factor has emerged as a game-changer for businesses aiming to thrive: sales enablement.

Sales enablement is no longer optional; it is essential. It's not just about occasional training sessions or distributing sales materials. Sales Enablement is a comprehensive, strategic function that aligns multiple teams, sales, marketing, product development, and leadership, around unified goals. This alignment equips sales teams with the tools, knowledge, and processes they need to close deals faster and consistently deliver results on a global scale.

In this chapter, we'll explore the evolving role of sales enablement, its integration into the broader business ecosystem, and why it's indispensable for achieving measurable growth. By the end, you will have an understanding how sales enablement drives performance, fosters team alignment, and propels businesses toward success.

THE EVOLUTION OF SALES ENABLEMENT

Traditionally, sales training was limited to sporadic workshops or quarterly content updates, leaving reps to navigate the complexities of the market on their own. However, the sales landscape has drastically changed due to:

- **Highly Informed Buyers:** Today's customers have access to a wealth of information, with 74% of buyers conducting more than half of their research online before making a purchase decision (Source: Forrester Research). With the evolution (revolution?) of collaborative generative AI support, buyers are now 'super informed' purchasers.

- **Longer Decision Cycles:** Complex products and services require more consideration, extending the sales cycle. Savvy buyers eek to understand product roadmaps and adjust their purchasing cycle accordingly.

- **Increased Competition:** Globalization and technological advancements have lowered barriers to entry, intensifying competition across industries. Localization is both imperative and much easier to achieve by utilizing the current tools.

These factors necessitate a proactive and strategic approach to supporting sales teams. Enter modern sales enablement.

FROM REACTIVE TO PROACTIVE SUPPORT

Sales enablement has evolved into a dynamic, ongoing process that anticipates the needs of sales reps and delivers solutions before challenges arise. Key elements supporting a successful process include:

- **Continuous Learning:** Moving beyond one-time training to regular, bite-sized learning modules that address current market challenges. A culture that promotes continuous learning enables the spacing and timing of learning to be optimized for increased engagement and retention. A study published in the Proceedings of the National Academy of Sciences found that spaced learning enhances and benefits memory retention (2019).

- **Cross-Team Alignment:** Ensuring consistent messaging and collaboration between sales, marketing, and product teams so reps can sell confidently and consultatively. When sales teams align with other functions, they not only achieve sales targets more predictably but also enhance customer satisfaction through coordinated efforts. Alignment ensures clarity of purpose and fosters a sense of unity and collective responsibility. This alignment perspective also serves as a powerful mechanism for discovering, cocreating, and delivering value to customers. Alignment allows teams to leverage diverse strengths and talents to build more trust-based customer relationships that drive mutual growth.

- **Real-Time Support:** Providing instant access to relevant content and coaching whenever and wherever reps need it. Real-time support can significantly improve performance and sales process efficiency By ensuring that relevant content, product details, and best practices can be retrieved quickly and consistently during live customer interactions, reps can provide accurate and timely responses. Thereby gaining trust with both your sales team and your potential customers. This support can foster team loyalty to your programs by offering faster resolutions to customer concerns and objections, which in turn may lead to shorter sales cycles and higher conversion rates.

WHY SALES ENABLEMENT MATTERS: REAL BUSINESS IMPACT

What makes sales enablement such a powerful driver of success? Its impact spans three critical areas, performance improvement, alignment across teams, and data-driven strategy.

Performance Improvement

Sales enablement programs enhance performance by equipping reps with actionable insights and skills to engage customers effectively. The results are tangible:

- **Higher Close Rates:** Reps are better prepared to handle objections and tailor solutions.

- **Faster Sales Cycles:** Efficient processes and readily available resources accelerate deal closure.

- **Improved Confidence:** Continuous learning boosts rep morale and competence.

  STATISTIC: Companies with a strong sales enablement function experience a 15% increase in win rates compared to those without one (Source: CSO Insights).

Alignment across Teams

One of the greatest challenges in organizations is misalignment between departments. Sales enablement bridges this gap by:

- **Unifying Messaging:** Ensuring that sales, marketing, and product teams communicate a consistent value proposition.

- **Facilitating Collaboration:** Creating channels for feedback and idea sharing across teams.

- **Enhancing Customer Experience:** Delivering a seamless journey from marketing materials to sales interactions.

Data-Driven Strategy

In the digital age, data is king. Sales enablement leverages metrics to:

- **Track Performance:** Monitoring key indicators like win rates, deal size, and sales cycle length.

- **Refine Strategies:** Using insights to adjust training programs and content.

- **Provide Timely Feedback:** Enabling reps to adapt their approach based on real-world data.

Understanding and utilizing your company's data tracking systems is imperative for the success of any enablement program.

REAL-WORLD BUSINESS CASE

The State of Sales Enablement Report 2023 provides highlights that organizations with dedicated enablement efforts see a 9%-point increase in average win rates.

Consider the example of Tech Global Solutions, a multinational software company facing stagnating sales despite a robust product line. By establishing a dedicated sales enablement function aligned with their business goals, they achieved remarkable results:

- **20% Increase in Sales Productivity:** Through continuous coaching and skill development.

- **30% Boost in Revenue:** By providing reps with real-time content and better customer insights.

- **Enhanced Customer Satisfaction:** Faster deal cycles and more personalized solutions improved client relationships.

What did they do differently?

- **Implemented Continuous Learning:** Regular training sessions kept reps updated on product changes and market trends.

- **Leveraged Data Analytics:** Performance metrics guided strategy adjustments and personalized coaching.

- **Aligned Teams:** Marketing and product teams worked closely with sales to ensure consistent messaging. The term "alignment" is used frequently in this book, because it is a major component of Kick A$$ Sales teams, and one that is often neglected because it requires time and skill. Build your expertise and comfort with "alignment"! It ensures achieving your end goal!

THE RESULT: Tech Global Solutions not only reversed their stagnation but also gained a competitive edge in the market.

THE STRATEGIC IMPERATIVE OF SALES ENABLEMENT

Sales enablement is more than training, it is about building a sustainable system that continuously elevates your sales organization's performance while aligning with overarching business strategies.

Key Benefits:

- **Reduced Time-to-Productivity:** New hires ramp-up faster, contributing to revenue sooner.

- **Consistent Target Achievement:** Teams regularly meet or exceed sales goals.

- **Increased Win Rates:** Well-equipped reps close more deals.

ASK YOURSELF: Can your organization afford to overlook the advantages that a robust sales enablement function provides?

CONCLUSION: EMBRACING SALES ENABLEMENT FOR GROWTH

In today's complex marketplace, sales enablement is not just a support function—it's a strategic necessity. It empowers sales teams, fosters cross-department collaboration, and drives measurable business outcomes.

As we delve deeper into this book, you'll learn how to:

- Build an effective sales enablement strategy from the ground up.

- Implement practical steps and frameworks for long term success.

- Leverage technology and data to continuously improve performance.

Ready to transform your sales organization?

The next chapter guides you through constructing a powerful sales enablement strategy.

CHAPTER SUMMARY

⇒ Sales Enablement Evolution: From reactive training to proactive, strategic support.

⇒ Impact Areas:
- *Performance Improvement*
- *Team Alignment*
- *Data-Driven Strategies*

⇒ Real-World Example: Tech Global Solutions' success story.

⇒ Strategic Necessity: Sales enablement as a key driver for growth.

CALL TO ACTION

☐ **REFLECT:** Assess your current sales support structures. Are they proactive or reactive?

☐ **ENGAGE:** Start your alignment conversations with cross-functional teams now.

☐ **PREPARE:** Baseline performance metrics are required for charting improvement.

By embracing sales enablement, you're not just improving your sales team—you're positioning your entire organization for sustainable growth and success.

FREQUENTLY ASKED QUESTIONS
The Critical Role of Sales Enablement in Today's Business Landscape

1. **What is sales enablement, and why is it important?**

   Sales enablement is a strategic, ongoing process that equips all client-facing employees with the tools, content, and information they need to engage buyers effectively. It is important because it enhances the efficiency and effectiveness of the sales team, leading to increased revenue, improved customer relationships, and a competitive advantage in the market.

2. **How does sales enablement differ from sales training?**

   While sales training is a component of sales enablement, focusing on skill development and knowledge transfer, sales enablement is broader. It encompasses training, content creation, technology implementation, and alignment between sales and other departments to support the entire sales process.

3. **What are the key challenges organizations face in implementing sales enablement?**

   Common challenges include lack of strategic alignment with business goals, inadequate technology integration, poor adoption by sales teams, insufficient measurement of impact, and difficulty scaling programs across the organization.

4. **How does sales enablement support the buyer's journey?**

   Sales enablement provides sales reps with the right content and insights at each stage of the buyer's journey, allowing them to engage prospects with relevant information, address their needs effectively, and guide them toward a purchase decision.

BUILD A KICKA$$ SALES TEAM

CHAPTER 2

CRAFTING A SALES ENABLEMENT STRATEGY FOR MEASURABLE RESULTS

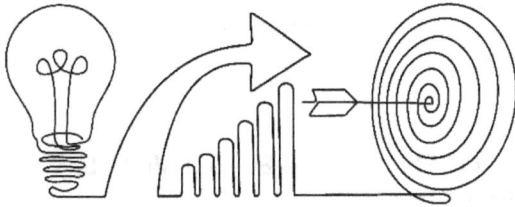

I n today's complex sales environment, the difference between a thriving sales team and a struggling one often comes down to one factor: strategy. Building a successful sales enablement strategy isn't about random training or sporadic content drops—it's about creating a structured, strategic plan that drives measurable business outcomes. When every sales interaction can make or break a deal, a well-crafted enablement strategy ensures your sales team is both prepared and empowered to excel.

This chapter guides you through the essential steps to develop a comprehensive sales enablement strategy that aligns with your business goals, addresses your team's specific needs, and sets the foundation for long-term success. By the end, you'll have a clear roadmap to transform your sales enablement efforts from ad hoc initiatives into a powerhouse of performance enhancement.

WHY A STRUCTURED SALES ENABLEMENT STRATEGY MATTERS

Without a structured approach, sales enablement efforts can become fragmented and ineffective. A clearly defined strategy ensures that every training session, piece of content, and coaching interaction serves a purpose aligned with overarching business objectives. Consider this: Companies with a formal sales enablement charter experience a 27.6% higher quota attainment rate than those without one (Source: Sales Enablement Pro).

CORE COMPONENTS OF AN EFFECTIVE SALES ENABLEMENT STRATEGY

Pillar 1: Cross-Functional Collaboration

Breaking down silos enhances efficiency and ensures everyone works toward the same goals. Effective collaboration begins with establishing clear communication channels and shared objectives across departments.

Strategies for Collaboration:

- **Regular Alignment Meetings:** Schedule cross-departmental meetings to share insights and updates

- **Shared KPIs:** Establish common performance indicators that encourage teamwork

- **Feedback Loops:** Create channels for sales reps to provide feedback to marketing and product teams

Moving from collaboration to content creation, let's examine how to develop materials that drive sales success.

Pillar 2: Content Development and Management

Content is the lifeblood of sales enablement, empowering reps to engage prospects with confidence and credibility.

Best Practices:

- **Consistency with Flexibility:** While maintaining brand consistency, incorporate fresh approaches to keep content engaging

- **Accessibility First:** Remove friction from content access while maintaining security

- **Interactive Elements:** Leverage modern tools like Synthesia. ai and the latest Camtasia for engaging video content

- **Regular Content Audits:** Implement systematic reviews to maintain relevance

With our content foundation established, let's explore how technology amplifies impact.

Pillar 3: Technology Integration

Before diving into specific technology recommendations, it's important to understand that the technology landscape is constantly evolving. Companies merge, new players emerge, and features change rapidly. The recommendations in this section reflect the market as of 2024, but by the time you're reading this, some details may have changed. What remains consistent, however, are the fundamental capabilities you should look for in each type of tool. Use these recommendations as a starting point for your research, focusing on the core functionalities that align with your specific needs rather than getting caught up with particular vendors.

When evaluating any technology solution, consider these evergreen factors:

- Integration capabilities with your existing systems

- Scalability to support your growth

- Security requirements and compliance standards

- Total cost of ownership, including implementation and training

- Vendor stability and support infrastructure

- User adoption potential based on interface design and ease of use

Tool Recommendations by Category:

CRM Platforms

- **Enterprise:** Salesforce ($150+/user/month)

  o **Best for:** Complex sales processes, large teams
  o **Integration complexity:** High
  o **Implementation time:** 3-6 months

- **Mid-market:** HubSpot ($800+/month for 10 users)

  o **Best for:** Growing companies, marketing alignment
  o **Integration complexity:** Medium
  o **Implementation time:** 1-3 months

- **Small Business:** Zoho ($14-52/user/month)

  o **Best for:** Budget-conscious teams

- Integration complexity: Low
- Implementation time: 2-4 weeks

Sales Enablement Platforms

Enterprise Solutions:

- Saleshood (Custom pricing)
  - **Best for:** Comprehensive sales training and coaching
  - **Minimum team size:** Can scale from 25 to 1000+
  - **Key strength:** Built-in video coaching and certification
  - **Integration complexity:** Medium
  - **Implementation time:** 2-3 months
  - **Notable feature:** Extensive peer learning capabilities

- Seismic ($100+/user/month)
  - **Best for:** Large content libraries, advanced analytics
  - **Minimum team size:** 50+
  - **Key strength:** LiveSend feature for document engagement tracking
  - **Integration complexity:** High
  - **Implementation time:** 3-4 months

Mid-market Solutions:

- Circle.so ($39-399/month based on plan)
  - **Best for:** Community-driven learning and collaboration
  - **Minimum team size:** Flexible, works for teams of all sizes
  - **Key strength:** Strong community engagement features

- Implementation time: 2-4 weeks
- Notable feature: White-label capability and custom domain options

- Showpad ($65+/user/month)

  - Best for: Training focus, content management
  - Minimum team size: 20+
  - Key strength: Integrated coaching and content analytics
  - Implementation time: 1-2 months

Growing Teams:

- Circle.so Essential Plan ($39/month)

  - Best for: Teams starting with community-based enablement
  - Minimum team size: No minimum
  - Key strength: Easy setup and management

- Saleshood Team Edition (Starting at $25/user/month)

  - Best for: Small teams needing core enablement features
  - Minimum team size: 5+
  - Key strength: Quick setup with essential features
  - Implementation time: 1-2 weeks
  - Implementation time: 1 week
  - Notable feature: Monetization capabilities for external training

- Spekit ($15+/user/month)

  - Best for: Just-in-time learning

- ○ **Minimum team size:** 10+
- ○ **Key strength:** Contextual learning within existing workflows
- ○ **Implementation time:** 1-2 weeks

With our technology foundation in place, let's examine how we measure and improve our efforts...

Pillar 4: Measurement and Continuous Improvement

Tracking performance ensures your strategy remains effective and evolves with changing needs.

Key Metrics to Monitor:

- **Time-to-Productivity:** How quickly new reps reach full performance

- **Win Rates:** Percentage of deals closed successfully

- **Sales Cycle Length:** Time taken to close deals

- **Content Utilization:** Which materials are used and their impact on sales

- **Rep Satisfaction:** Feedback from sales teams on enablement initiatives

STEP-BY-STEP GUIDE TO BUILDING YOUR STRATEGY

Step 1: Align with Business Goals (Estimated time: 2-3 weeks)

Begin by understanding and documenting how sales enablement will support each business objective. Hold focused workshops with leadership to ensure alignment.

Questions to Consider:

- What are our revenue targets for the next year?

- Which products or services are we focusing on?

- What market segments are we targeting?

Step 2: Conduct a Needs Assessment (Estimated time: 3-4 weeks)

Systematically identify gaps in skills, processes, and resources through surveys, interviews, and data analysis.

Assessment Areas:

- **Skill Gaps:** Use surveys or assessments to gauge proficiency in key sales competencies

- **Process Bottlenecks:** Analyze the sales workflow to identify inefficiencies

- **Content Needs:** Gather input from reps on the usefulness of current materials

Step 3: Build Your Cross-Functional Team (Estimated time: 1-2 weeks)

Assemble key stakeholders from sales, marketing, product, and customer success teams. Establish clear roles and responsibilities.

Team Members Should Include:

- **Sales Leaders:** Provide insights into team needs and priorities

- **Marketing Professionals:** Ensure alignment on messaging and content

- **Product Experts:** Offer deep knowledge of product features and roadmaps

- **Customer Success Teams:** Share feedback on customer experiences and pain points

Step 4: Develop Content and Training Roadmap (Estimated time: 4-6 weeks)

Create a detailed timeline for content creation, training programs, and technology implementation.

Roadmap Elements:

- **Training Schedule:** Outline topics, formats, and frequency

- **Content Creation:** Plan for developing or updating materials

- **Technology Implementation:** Schedule rollouts of new tools or platforms

Step 5: Implement Technology Solutions (Estimated time: 8-12 weeks)

Select and integrate tools that support your strategy, following a phased approach to ensure successful adoption.

Implementation Tips:

- **Pilot Programs:** Test new tools with a small group before full deployment
- **User Training:** Provide comprehensive training to ensure adoption
- **Integration:** Work with IT to integrate tools for seamless data flow

Step 6: Establish Metrics and KPIs (Estimated time: 2-3 weeks)

Define success metrics aligned with business objectives. Implement KPI tracking for:

- Win rates
- Content usage
- Time to productivity
- Active user engagement
- Training completion rates

Step 7: Foster Continuous Learning (Ongoing)

Create systems and processes that encourage ongoing development and adaptation.

CONCLUSION: SETTING THE STAGE FOR SUCCESS

By following these steps and implementing the recommended tools and frameworks, you're creating a foundation for sustainable sales success. Remember, strategy implementation is not a one-time event. This is an ongoing process of refinement and improvement.

FREQUENTLY ASKED QUESTIONS

1. **What are the essential components of an effective sales enablement strategy?**

   An effective strategy includes clear alignment with business goals, understanding of the sales team's needs, defined objectives and KPIs, a plan for content and training development, technology integration, and a process for measuring and iterating on results.

2. **How do I align sales enablement initiatives with business objectives?**

   Begin by understanding the organization's overall goals, such as revenue targets, market expansion, or customer retention. Then, design sales enablement programs that directly support these goals, ensuring that every initiative has a clear connection to business outcomes.

3. **What KPIs should I use to measure the success of my sales enablement programs?**

   KPIs may include sales productivity metrics (e.g., quota attainment, win rates), training completion rates, content usage statistics, time-to-productivity for new hires, and qualitative feedback from the sales team.

4. **How often should I revisit and adjust my sales enablement strategy?**

Regularly assessing your strategy, quarterly at minimum, ensures that training stays aligned with evolving business objectives, market conditions, and feedback from the sales team. Be ready to adapt and iterate when necessary to sustain a positive impact.

CHAPTER SUMMARY

→ A well-planned strategy is essential for impactful sales enablement

→ Core components include cross-functional collaboration, content development, technology integration, and measurement

→ Implementation requires careful planning and stakeholder buy-in

→ Regular assessment and adjustment ensure continued effectiveness

→ Success metrics should align with business objectives

CALL TO ACTION

☐ Review your current sales enablement efforts for gaps and opportunities

☐ Schedule meetings with key stakeholders to begin collaboration

☐ Start drafting your content and training roadmap with clear timelines

By proactively developing and implementing a strategic sales enablement plan, you're investing in the growth and competitiveness of your organization. The steps you take today will pave the way for a more agile, informed, and successful sales team tomorrow.

FREQUENTLY ASKED QUESTIONS
Crafting a Sales Enablement Strategy for Measurable Results

1. **What are the essential components of an effective sales enablement strategy?**

An effective strategy includes clear alignment with business goals, understanding of the sales team's needs, defined objectives and KPIs, a plan for content and training development, technology integration, and a process for measuring and iterating on results.

2. **How do I align sales enablement initiatives with business objectives?**

Begin by understanding the organization's overall goals, such as revenue targets, market expansion, or customer retention. Then, design sales enablement programs that directly support these goals, ensuring that every initiative has a clear connection to business outcomes.

When we built the Systems Selling Academy, we held monthly meetings that became weekly as we got closer to launch. These meetings were attended by all the cross-functional teams involved. We had weekly small meeting touchpoints, and daily standups depending on the stage we were working on.

Communications were weekly and shared across all of the large team intended participants. We all kept aligned and aware of progress and concerns on a shared doc that everyone had read/write and view permissions.

3. **What KPIs should I use to measure the success of my sales enablement programs?**

   KPIs may include sales productivity metrics (e.g., quota attainment, win rates), training completion rates, content usage statistics, time-to-productivity for new hires, and qualitative feedback from the sales team.

   We set up a weekly Excel spreadsheet that was color coded to display individual and team completion percentages, that was shared with managers and senior leadership. Knowing that there was high-level oversight on engagement kept the team energized. Top performing teams were verbally recognized at company meetings and received incentives quarterly.

4. **How often should I revisit and adjust my sales enablement strategy?**

   Regularly assessing your strategy, quarterly at minimum, ensures that training stays aligned with evolving business objectives, market conditions, and feedback from the sales team. Be ready to adapt and iterate when necessary to sustain a positive impact.

CHAPTER 3

BUILDING A SALES ENABLEMENT TECH STACK FOR OPTIMAL PERFORMANCE

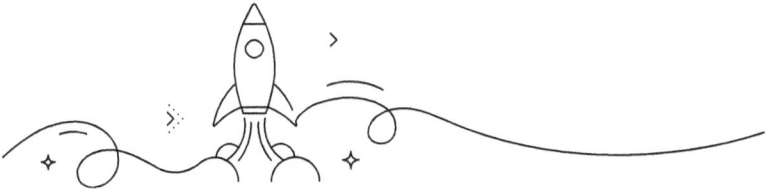

I n the digital age, technology isn't just a tool, it's a strategic asset that can make or break your sales enablement efforts. While Chapter 2 introduced the core technology components needed for sales enablement, this chapter delves deeper into how to strategically build, integrate, and optimize your tech stack to create a cohesive ecosystem that drives measurable results.

BEYOND INDIVIDUAL TOOLS: CREATING AN INTEGRATED ECOSYSTEM

A successful sales enablement tech stack is greater than the sum of its parts. Rather than focusing on individual tools, we need to understand how different technologies work together to support the entire sales journey. When properly integrated, your tech stack becomes a force multiplier, enhancing every aspect of your sales enablement strategy.

CONSIDER THIS: Companies with highly integrated tech stacks see a 50% higher sales quota attainment compared to those with disconnected tools (Source: Aberdeen Group). This dramatic difference comes not from the tools themselves, but from how they work together to create a seamless experience for both sales teams and customers.

FRAMEWORK FOR BUILDING YOUR TECH STACK

Step 1: Map Your Sales Process

Before selecting any new tools, you need a clear understanding of your sales process workflows. This mapping exercise reveals opportunities for technological enhancement and automation.

Questions to guide your mapping:

- Where do your sales representatives spend most of their time?

- What tasks are repetitive and could be automated?

- Where do bottlenecks occur in your current process?

- What information do reps need at each stage of the sale?

For example, if your mapping reveals that reps spend three hours per week scheduling follow-up emails, this indicates a clear opportunity for automation through a sales engagement platform.

Step 2: Define Your Technology Requirements

Requirements gathering should focus on solving specific business problems rather than chasing features. Start with these fundamental questions:

Process Requirements:

- Which stages of your sales process need the most support?

- What data needs to flow between different systems?

- How will different departments need to access and use the tools?

Technical Requirements:

- What security standards must be met?

- Which existing systems need integration?

- What scalability requirements should be considered?

User Requirements:

- What is your team's technical proficiency level?

- How much training time can realistically be allocated?

- What are the must-have features versus nice-to-have features?

Step 3: Integration Planning

Integration planning is crucial for creating a cohesive tech stack. Think of your tech stack as an orchestra—each instrument must play in harmony with the others to create beautiful music.

Key Integration Considerations:

- **Data Flow:** Map how information will move between systems

- **API Limitations:** Understand what each system can and cannot do

- **Authentication:** Plan how users will access multiple systems

- **Backup Procedures:** Establish how data will be protected across integrated systems

Step 4: Change Management Strategy

Technology implementation success depends more on people than on the tools themselves. Your change management strategy should address:

Preparation Phase:

- Communication planning

- Stakeholder mapping

- Resistance identification

- Training needs assessment

Implementation Phase:

- Pilot program design

- Feedback collection mechanisms

- Success metrics definition

- Support system establishment

Step 5: Optimization Framework

Continuous optimization ensures your tech stack evolves with your organization. Establish these key elements:

Monitoring Systems:

- Usage analytics

- Performance metrics

- User feedback channels

- System health checks

Review Cycles:

- **Weekly:** Basic usage metrics and immediate issues

- **Monthly:** Performance trends and user adoption

- **Quarterly:** Strategic alignment and ROI assessment

- **Annual:** Comprehensive stack evaluation

EMERGING TECHNOLOGIES IN SALES ENABLEMENT

While Chapter 2 covered core technologies, let's explore emerging technologies that are reshaping sales enablement:

Artificial Intelligence Integration

AI is transforming how we approach sales enablement through:

Conversational Intelligence: Advanced AI systems can analyze sales conversations to provide insights on:

- Successful closing techniques

- Common customer objections

- Effective discovery questions

- Coaching opportunities

Predictive Analytics: Modern AI tools can:

- Forecast deal outcomes

- Suggest next best actions

- Identify at-risk opportunities

- Recommend optimal pricing strategies

Virtual Reality (VR) and Augmented Reality (AR)

These technologies are creating new possibilities for sales training:

- Virtual product demonstrations

- Immersive role-playing scenarios

- Remote collaboration environments

- Interactive product visualization

BUILDING FOR THE FUTURE: FUTURE-PROOFING YOUR TECH STACK

Technology evolves rapidly, and your tech stack needs to be adaptable. Consider these principles for future-proofing:

Architecture Principles:

- Modular design for easy component replacement
- API-first approach for flexibility
- Cloud-native solutions for scalability
- Data portability between systems

Innovation Management:

- Regular technology landscape reviews
- Pilot programs for emerging technologies
- Innovation budget allocation
- Cross-functional innovation teams

CONCLUSION: CREATING YOUR TECHNOLOGY ROADMAP

Success with sales enablement technology isn't about having the latest tools—it's about creating a coherent ecosystem that supports your sales process and scales with your organization. As you build your tech stack, remember that technology should enable, not complicate, your sales process.

CHAPTER SUMMARY

→ Integration is more important than individual tool selection

→ Change management determines implementation success

→ Continuous optimization ensures long-term value

→ Emerging technologies offer new possibilities

→ Future-proofing requires strategic planning

CALL TO ACTION

Start building your technology roadmap by:

☐ Mapping your current sales process in detail

☐ Identifying your biggest technology pain points

☐ Creating an integration plan for existing tools

☐ Developing a change management strategy

The next chapter will explore how to bring your sales enablement vision to life by developing engaging programs that resonate with your team and drive real results.

FREQUENTLY ASKED QUESTIONS
Building a Sales Enablement Tech Stack for Optimal Performance

1. **How do I ensure my tech stack remains integrated as we add new tools?**

   Start with a strong integration framework that defines how new tools must connect with your existing systems. Establish clear requirements for API capabilities, data synchronization, and user authentication before adopting any new technology. Regular integration audits help identify potential issues before they become problems.

2. **What's the best way to handle resistance to new technology implementation?**

   Address resistance through a combination of clear communication, demonstrable benefits, and phased implementation. Start by identifying and involving influential team members early in the process. Show concrete examples of how the technology will make their jobs easier. Provide ample training and support, and celebrate early wins to build momentum.

3. **How can I measure the ROI of my sales enablement tech stack?**

   Track both quantitative and qualitative metrics. Quantitative measures include reduced administrative time, increased deal velocity, and improved win rates. Qualitative measures might include user satisfaction, ease of accessing information, and improved collaboration. Compare these against your baseline measurements from before implementation to demonstrate value.

4. **What are the warning signs that my tech stack needs optimization?**

   Watch for indicators like declining usage rates, increasing complaints about tool complexity, data inconsistencies between systems, or sales reps creating workarounds. Also monitor for redundant functionalities across different tools and rising maintenance costs. These signs suggest it's time to evaluate and optimize your stack.

5. **How do I balance innovation with stability in my tech stack?**

   Create a structured innovation process that includes regular evaluation of new technologies while maintaining core system stability. Dedicate a portion of your budget to testing new tools through controlled pilot programs. This way you can ensure new additions provide significant value beyond existing solutions and integrate well with your core systems.

CHAPTER 4

BRINGING YOUR SALES ENABLEMENT VISION TO LIFE

H aving a well-crafted sales enablement strategy and the right technology in place is essential, but without effective implementation, even the best-laid plans can falter. The real challenge lies in translating your vision into engaging, impactful programs that resonate with your sales team and drive measurable results.

In this chapter, we'll delve into practical steps to bring your sales enablement vision to life. We'll explore how to design programs that cater to different learning styles, incorporate the SEID framework for optimized instructional design, and deliver training that is both inclusive and engaging. Real-world examples and actionable insights will guide you in creating programs that not only educate but also inspire your sales team to reach new heights.

FROM VISION TO ACTION: THE IMPLEMENTATION JOURNEY

Turning strategy into action involves careful planning and execution.

Key Steps:

1. *Define Clear Objectives:* What specific outcomes do you want to achieve?

2. *Understand Your Audience:* Tailor programs to meet the needs of different learner profiles.

3. *Apply the SEID Framework:* Utilize the Specific, Engaging, Interactive, Design approach for optimized instructional design.

4. *Choose the Right Modalities:* Select training formats that align with your content and audience.

5. *Leverage Technology Wisely:* Use tools and platforms that enhance learning without adding unnecessary complexity.

6. *Measure and Iterate:* Continuously assess effectiveness and make improvements.

DESIGNING ENGAGING AND EFFECTIVE PROGRAMS

Step 1. Define Clear Objectives

Set specific, measurable goals for your programs.

SMART Goals Framework:

- **Specific:** Clearly define what you want to achieve.

- **Measurable:** Identify how you will measure success.

- **Achievable:** Ensure goals are realistic.

- **Relevant:** Align with broader business objectives.

- **Time-Bound:** Set deadlines for achieving goals.

  SMART EXAMPLE: Increase product knowledge proficiency among sales reps by 20% within three months, as measured by assessment scores.

Step 2. Understand Your Audience

Different reps have different learning preferences.

Learner Profiles:

- **Visual Learners:** Prefer images, diagrams, videos.

- **Auditory Learners:** Benefit from discussions, podcasts.

- **Kinesthetic Learners:** Learn by doing through simulations and role-plays.

- **Reading/Writing Learners:** Prefer written materials and note-taking.

Action Steps:

- **Conduct Surveys:** Gather information on preferred learning styles.

- **Segment Your Audience:** Group learners based on experience levels, roles, or learning preferences.

Step 3. Apply the appropriate Instructional Design Framework for Optimized Program Design

Actionable Frameworks for Sales Enablement Success

Building a successful sales enablement program isn't just about concepts; it's about action. To truly empower your sales teams, it is crucial to offer actionable frameworks that can be immediately applied to improve performance, foster alignment, and drive growth. Below are key frameworks to elevate your sales enablement strategy from planning to execution.

The EMPOWER Model

The EMPOWER model serves as a blueprint to create engaging and impactful enablement initiatives:

- **Engage Early:** Generate excitement from the outset by involving stakeholders and sales reps in the planning phase. When sales teams feel a sense of ownership, they are more committed to the process.

- **Make It Relevant:** Tailor your training content to the unique needs of your reps. Align training objectives with real business challenges to keep it meaningful and impactful.

- **Provide Support:** Build coaching opportunities into your programs. Create coaching cohorts or assign mentors to help reps put their learning into practice.

- **Open Communication:** Encourage dialogue throughout the enablement process. Sales reps should feel comfortable giving feedback, sharing insights, and asking questions.

- **Win Together:** Celebrate achievements, both big and small. Recognition fosters motivation and reinforces the importance of the program.

- **Evolve Continuously:** Your enablement strategy should adapt to changing business conditions. Collect data and feedback regularly to iterate and improve your programs.

- **Reinforce Learning:** Provide multiple opportunities for reinforcement through follow-up activities, quizzes, and coaching sessions to solidify knowledge.

The SCALE Framework for Growth

Scaling your enablement efforts requires a structured approach that ensures consistent results across teams and regions. The SCALE framework focuses on five key pillars:

- **Standardize Core Processes:** Develop and document key enablement processes so that they can be repeated effectively across teams. Consistency is crucial to scale efficiently.

- **Customize for Local Needs:** Adapt core training content to meet the cultural and market-specific requirements of different regions. Customization ensures the program remains relevant and engaging.

- **Automate Where Possible:** Leverage AI technology to automate repetitive tasks like content distribution and progress tracking. Automation helps free up time for more strategic activities.

- **Leverage Cross-Functional Collaboration:** Successful scaling requires buy-in and input from multiple teams, including marketing, product, and customer success. Establish regular touchpoints to foster alignment.

- **Evaluate and Refine:** Track key performance indicators (KPIs) such as content usage, win rates, and time-to-productivity to measure effectiveness and identify areas for improvement.

The SEID Instructional Design Approach

The SEID (Specific, Engaging, Interactive, Design) framework is designed to make training effective, non-boring, and tailored to the needs of your sales team. This is my preferred actionable favorite!

- **Specific:** Ensure that every training initiative has clearly defined goals. Know the exact skill gap you're addressing and tailor content to fill that gap.

- **Engaging:** Keep your sales reps engaged through storytelling, real-life case studies, and examples that are directly relevant to their day-to-day activities.

- **Interactive:** Make learning hands-on. Use role-playing exercises, simulations, and group activities to encourage participation and build practical skills.

- **Design:** Thoughtful design is key. Make sure your training is accessible to everyone and visually appealing. Use visuals, infographics, and videos to support different learning styles.

ADDIE for Enablement Implementation

The classic ADDIE (Analyze, Design, Develop, Implement, Evaluate) model is perfectly suited for developing and rolling out sales enablement programs:

- **Analyze:** Identify gaps in sales skills, knowledge, and resources. Use data to determine what's working and what isn't.

- **Design:** Develop a strategic plan to address these gaps. Define learning objectives, delivery methods, and content structure.

- **Develop:** Create training content, toolkits, and resources. Collaborate with subject matter experts (SMEs) to ensure accuracy and relevance.

- **Implement:** Roll out the program in phases. Start with pilot groups to gather insights and make adjustments before full deployment.

- **Evaluate:** Measure the program's success. Gather feedback from participants and analyze performance metrics to understand the impact and identify opportunities for improvement.

CLIMB for Continual Learning

The CLIMB framework is designed to encourage continuous learning and growth among sales teams:

- **Curiosity-Driven Learning:** Foster a culture of curiosity by encouraging reps to explore topics beyond their immediate responsibilities.

- **Leverage Learning Moments:** Integrate learning opportunities into daily workflows. Short quizzes, learning breaks, and spontaneous peer coaching moments can help keep learning fresh.

- **Incentivize Participation:** Reward reps for engaging in learning activities. Gamification, public recognition, and tangible rewards can motivate teams to embrace learning.

- **Measure Impact:** Use metrics to track how learning initiatives translate to performance improvements. Metrics like lead conversion rates, win rates, and average deal size can indicate learning success.

- **Build on Wins:** Reinforce successful behaviors. When a learning initiative leads to positive results, celebrate it and replicate it across the team.

Bringing It All Together

These actionable frameworks—EMPOWER, SCALE, SEID, ADDIE, and CLIMB—provide a comprehensive approach to designing, scaling, and continuously improving sales enablement initiatives. Each one addresses a different aspect of enablement, from engagement and instructional design to scaling and fostering continuous growth. Use these frameworks to create a well-rounded enablement strategy that not only trains your sales reps but equips them to be agile, boldly curious, and consistently high-performing.

By employing these frameworks, your sales enablement efforts can truly transform from simple training programs to impactful, growth-driving initiatives that deliver measurable business results.

Applying the SEID Framework: A Deep Dive

Designing impactful sales enablement programs requires a structured approach that ensures training is not only informative but also engaging and actionable. Let me share how the SEID (Specific, Engaging, Interactive, Design) framework came to life.

The Genesis of SEID

While mentoring early career Instructional Designers, I noticed a recurring challenge: bridging the gap between instructional design principles and the practical needs of sales enablement. These talented individuals often grappled with tailoring their educational expertise to meet the fast-paced, results-driven environment of sales teams.

Recognizing this need, I developed the SEID framework as a guide to help Instructional Designers create training programs that are:

- Specific to the needs of the sales team.

- Engaging to capture and hold attention.

- Interactive to promote active learning.

- Thoughtfully Designed to be inclusive and accessible.

By applying SEID, these Instructional Designers could more effectively contribute to the success of sales enablement initiatives, ensuring that training was both impactful and aligned with organizational goals.

Bringing SEID into Sales Enablement

The positive outcomes from mentoring sessions and the application of SEID in various projects underscored its effectiveness. This inspired me to integrate the framework into broader sales enablement strategies, helping organizations develop training programs that truly resonate with their sales teams.

Overview of the SEID Framework

1. Specific

2. Engaging

3. Interactive

4. Design

Let's delve into each component to understand how it contributes to effective sales enablement instructional design.

Specific

Know the specifics of:

- **The Ask for the Training Request:** Clearly define the objectives. What are the goals of the training? What problems are you aiming to solve?

- **The Why of This Request:** Understand the underlying reasons. Is it to address a skills gap, introduce a new product, or improve sales techniques?

- **The Stakeholders:** Identify who has a vested interest—executives, sales managers, team leads.

- **The Audience:** Know your learners' roles, experience levels, and learning preferences.

APPLICATION IN PRACTICE: Before developing any training program, gather detailed information. For example, if the sales team is struggling with closing deals, determine whether the issue lies in negotiation skills, product knowledge, or understanding customer needs. This specificity ensures the training is targeted and relevant.

ACTION STEPS:

- ☐ **Conduct Needs Assessments:** Use surveys, interviews, and performance data to pinpoint exact training needs.

- ☐ **Set Clear Objectives:** Define SMART goals for the training program.

- ☐ **Align with Business Goals:** Ensure the training supports broader organizational objectives.

Engaging

Confirm there is in-depth engagement with:

- **Stakeholders:** Involve key stakeholders throughout the design process to ensure alignment and buy-in.

- **Subject Matter Experts (SMEs):** Collaborate with experts to develop accurate and insightful content.

- **The Context of the Content:** Ensure material is relevant to real-world scenarios the sales team encounters.

- **The Targeted Audience:** Tailor content to the audience's needs and existing knowledge.

- **Metrics and Analytics:** Define how you will measure engagement and effectiveness.

- **Delivery Methodologies and Technology Platforms:** Choose platforms and methods that enhance engagement (discussed in Step 4).

APPLICATION IN PRACTICE: Engaging training captures learners' attention and keeps them invested. Incorporating storytelling and real-life case studies can make content more relatable. Using platforms like Circle.so can facilitate community discussions and peer engagement.

ACTION STEPS:

☐ **Incorporate Multimedia Elements:** Use videos, animations, and infographics to make content visually appealing.

☐ **Interactive Sessions:** Include group discussions, Q&A segments, and collaborative activities.

☐ **Feedback Mechanisms:** Provide opportunities for learners to give and receive feedback.

Interactive

Ensure Interactivity with:

- **Sticky, Consumable, Non-Boring Content:** Design content that is memorable and easy to digest.

- **Actionable Relevant Content:** Provide practical steps that learners can apply immediately.

- **Appropriate Complexity Level:** Match the content's difficulty to the audience's expertise.

- **Assessments That Matter:** Develop evaluations that test understanding and encourage application.

  APPLICATION IN PRACTICE: Interactive training increases retention and encourages active learning. Simulations or role-playing exercises allow sales reps to practice new techniques in a risk-free environment.

ACTION STEPS:

- ☐ **Use Interactive Tools:** Implement quizzes, polls, and gamification elements.

- ☐ **Encourage Participation:** Design activities that require learner input and collaboration.

- ☐ **Provide Real-Time Feedback:** Offer immediate responses to assessments and exercises.

Design

Confirm the Design is:

- **Inclusive in Language and Engagement:** Use language that is accessible and considerate of diverse backgrounds.

- **Appeals to Diversity Within Your Targeted Audience:** Recognize and address different cultures, experiences, and perspectives.

- **Simple:** Keep designs clean and uncluttered to enhance focus and comprehension.

- **Capable of Providing Reports to Stakeholders and Feedback to Participants:** Utilize systems that track progress and enable reporting.

APPLICATION IN PRACTICE: An effective design ensures that training is accessible and meaningful to all participants. Designing content with universal design principles allows learners with varying abilities and learning styles to engage fully.

ACTION STEPS:

- ☐ **Apply Instructional Design Principles:** Use models like ADDIE (Analyze, Design, Develop, Implement, Evaluate) to structure your approach.

- ☐ **Ensure Accessibility:** Comply with accessibility standards (e.g., WCAG) to make content usable by everyone.

- ☐ **Utilize Analytics:** Leverage LMS platforms to track engagement and performance, providing data to stakeholders.

Implementing the SEID Framework: A Practical Example

Imagine you're tasked with developing a training program to improve your sales team's proficiency in selling a new product line. Here's how you might apply the SEID framework:

1. Specific:

- o **Define Objectives:** Increase product knowledge and sales confidence by 30% within three months.
- o **Understand the Audience:** Sales reps with varying levels of experience in the product category.

2. Engaging:

- o **Collaborate with SMEs:** Work with product managers to gather in-depth information.
- o **Choose Platforms:** Utilize interactive webinars and an online community via Circle.so for discussions.

3. Interactive:

- o **Develop Simulations:** Create role-play scenarios where reps practice pitching the new product.
- o **Assessments:** Incorporate quizzes with instant feedback to reinforce learning.

4. Design:

- o **Inclusive Content:** Ensure examples and language are culturally sensitive and relevant.
- o **Simplicity:** Use clear visuals and concise text to facilitate understanding.
- o **Reporting:** Set up dashboards to monitor progress and share results with stakeholders.

Step 4. Choose the Right Training Modalities

Select formats that best deliver your content.

Training Modalities:

- **Instructor-Led Training (ILT):** In-person or virtual classrooms for interactive learning.

- **eLearning Modules:** Self-paced online courses for flexibility.

- **Webinars and Virtual Workshops:** Combine visual and auditory learning with real-time interaction.

- **Microlearning:** Short, focused lessons that fit into busy schedules.

- **Blended Learning:** A combination of modalities for a comprehensive approach.

- **Learning Path:** Recommended series of learning to gain competency on a specific topic or set of topics. Can lead to Certifications.

- **Certifications:** Allows the completion of an entire learning flow. Let's management track fully trained team members. Provides team pride, establishes policies and standards of knowledge about the company, product, sales policies, and more.

TIP: Use blended learning to cater to multiple learning styles and reinforce concepts.

Step 5. Leverage Technology Wisely

Integrate technology to enhance, not complicate, learning.

Emerging Technologies:

- **Artificial Intelligence (AI):** Continually evolving.

  - **Personalized Learning Paths:** AI can tailor content based on individual progress.

  - **Chatbots and Virtual Coaches:** Provide instant support and feedback.

  - **Predictive Analytics:** Identify at-risk learners and offer proactive interventions.

- **Virtual Reality (VR) and Augmented Reality (AR):**

  - **Immersive Simulations:** Allow reps to practice in realistic scenarios.

  - **Interactive Product Demos:** Enhance understanding of complex products.

Best Practices:

- **Start Small:** Pilot new technologies with a select group.

- **Ensure Accessibility:** Technology should be easy to use and accessible to all team members.

- **Maintain Human Touch:** Technology should augment, not replace, human interaction.

Step 6. Deliver Inclusive and Accessible Training

Ensure your programs are accessible to all team members.

Strategies for Inclusivity:

- **Use Clear Language:** Avoid jargon and complex terms. Use inclusive language and inclusive visuals.

- **Provide Multiple Formats:** Offer materials in written, audio, and visual formats.

- **Ensure Accessibility Compliance:** Follow guidelines like the Web Content Accessibility Guidelines (WCAG).

- **Foster an Inclusive Environment:** Encourage participation from all team members and respect diverse perspectives.

CASE STUDY: A global company implemented training materials in multiple languages and saw a significant increase in engagement across regions. Leverage generative AI tools to easily localize content.

Best Practices for Engaging Virtual Training

With remote work becoming more prevalent, virtual training is essential.

Make It Interactive

Engage participants actively.

Techniques:

- **Polls and Quizzes:** Use tools like Mentimeter or Kahoot to gather input.

- **Breakout Rooms:** Facilitate small group discussions and activities.

- **Live Chat and Q&A:** Encourage questions and real-time interaction.

Incorporate Storytelling

Stories make content memorable.

Approach:

- **Use Real Examples:** Share success stories and lessons learned.
- **Create Scenarios:** Develop relatable situations that reps might face.

Encourage Collaboration

Foster peer learning.

Methods:

- **Group Projects:** Assign tasks that require teamwork.
- **Peer Coaching:** Pair up reps to support each other's learning.

Provide Resources for Self-Paced Learning

Allow reps to learn at their own pace.

Resources:

- **On-Demand Videos:** Record sessions for later viewing.
- **Digital Libraries:** Provide access to articles, guides, and toolkits.

Real-World Example: Implementing the SEID Framework at Tech Global Solutions

COMPANY: Tech Global Solutions

CHALLENGE: The sales team was struggling to effectively sell a new product line due to insufficient product knowledge and low confidence.

Solution:

1. *Specific:*

   o **Objectives:** Increase product knowledge by 30% and improve sales confidence within three months.

   o **Audience:** Sales reps across various regions with different experience levels.

2. *Engaging:*

   o **Stakeholder Involvement:** Collaborated with product managers and regional sales leaders.

   o **Content Relevance:** Included region-specific case studies and examples.

   o **Platforms:** Used Circle.so for community discussions and peer support.

3. *Interactive:*

   o **Simulations:** Developed virtual role-play exercises mimicking customer interactions.

   o **Assessments:** Implemented quizzes with immediate feedback and leaderboards to encourage friendly competition.

4. *Design:*

- ○ **Inclusivity:** Ensured content was culturally sensitive and available in multiple languages.
- ○ **Simplicity:** Used clear visuals and concise messaging.
- ○ **Reporting:** Set up dashboards to track progress and share insights with stakeholders.

Results:

- **Knowledge Increase:** Assessment scores improved by 35% on average.

- **Sales Confidence:** Reps reported a significant boost in confidence during customer interactions.

- **Sales Performance:** Achieved a 25% increase in sales of the new product line within four months.

CONCLUSION: BRINGING YOUR VISION TO LIFE WITH SEID

By applying the SEID framework, you can transform your sales enablement vision into effective, impactful programs that resonate with your sales team. Focusing on specificity, engagement, interactivity, and thoughtful design ensures that your training is not only informative but also transformative.

Key Takeaways:

- **Personal Experience Shapes Success:** The SEID framework was born out of real-world challenges and mentoring experiences, highlighting the importance of practical application.

- **Customization is Crucial:** Tailor programs to meet the specific needs of your team using the SEID framework.

- **Engagement Drives Adoption:** Interactive and relevant content increases participation and retention.

- **Technology Enhances Learning:** Use tools that add value without overcomplicating the experience.

- **Continuous Improvement:** Regularly assess and refine your programs for sustained success.

Are you ready to transform your sales enablement vision into actionable, impactful programs?

In the next chapter, we'll explore strategies to drive engagement and motivation within your sales team, ensuring your enablement efforts translate into tangible performance improvements.

CHAPTER SUMMARY

⇒ Implementation Steps: From defining objectives to measuring success.

⇒ SEID Framework: A practical methodology for designing effective training programs.
  - *Specific*
  - *Engaging*
  - *Interactive*
  - *Design*

⇒ Program Design: Aligning modalities and content with learner needs.

⇒ Technology Use: Leveraging AI and other tools thoughtfully.

⇒ Inclusivity and Accessibility: Ensuring all team members can fully participate.

→ Real-World Success: Tech Global Solutions' effective program rollout.

INTERACTIVE REFLECTIVE QUESTIONS

1. *Application of SEID:* How can you apply the SEID framework to your current or upcoming training initiatives?

2. *Personal Inspiration:* Reflect on your own experiences. How might challenges you've faced inspire innovative solutions?

3. *Audience Understanding:* What steps can you take to better understand the specific needs and preferences of your sales team?

4. *Engagement Strategies:* Which engaging and interactive elements will resonate most with your team?

5. *Design Considerations:* How will you ensure your training design is inclusive and accessible to all participants?

6. *Technology Integration:* What technologies can you leverage to enhance your training programs without adding unnecessary complexity?

CALL TO ACTION

☐ Assess Your Current Programs: Start today by evaluating your current training programs against the SEID framework and identify one area to enhance with a new approach. Small changes can lead to big results!

☐ Evaluate how well your existing training aligns with the SEID framework.

☐ Leverage Personal Experiences: Consider how your own challenges and successes can inform your approach to sales enablement.

☐ Plan Your Next Training: Use the SEID framework to design your next sales enablement program.

☐ Gather Feedback: Solicit input from your sales team to continuously improve your approach.

☐ Share Your Success: Encourage knowledge sharing within your organization about effective training practices.

By effectively bringing your sales enablement vision to life using the SEID framework, you empower your sales team with the skills, knowledge, and motivation they need to excel in today's competitive market.

FREQUENTLY ASKED QUESTIONS
Bringing Your Sales Enablement Vision to Life

1. **What is the SEID framework, and how does it benefit my training programs?**

   The SEID (Specific, Engaging, Interactive, Design) framework is a methodology for creating effective sales training programs. It ensures that training is tailored to specific needs, engaging for learners, interactive to promote active participation, and thoughtfully designed to be inclusive and accessible.

2. **How can I apply the SEID framework in practice?**

   Specific: Clearly define training objectives, understand the "why," identify stakeholders, and know your audience.

Engaging: Involve stakeholders and SMEs, make content relevant, and choose appropriate delivery methods.

Interactive: Use sticky, consumable content, actionable materials, suitable complexity levels, and meaningful assessments.

Design: Ensure inclusivity, appeal to diversity, maintain simplicity, and provide reporting capabilities.

3. **What are the best practices for delivering virtual training effectively?**

Make virtual training interactive through polls, quizzes, and breakout sessions. Incorporate storytelling, encourage collaboration, provide resources for self-paced learning, and leverage technology platforms that facilitate engagement.

4. **How do I ensure my training programs are inclusive and accessible?**

Use clear and inclusive language, offer materials in multiple formats (text, audio, visual), comply with accessibility standards (e.g., WCAG), and design content that respects and reflects the diversity of your audience.

CHAPTER 5

DRIVING ENGAGEMENT AND MOTIVATION IN SALES ENABLEMENT

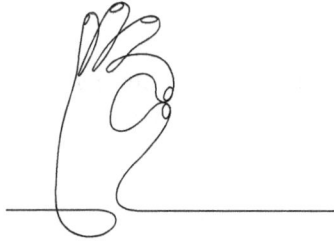

In the world of sales, knowledge alone isn't enough. It is the application of that knowledge that leads to success. For your sales enablement initiatives to truly make an impact, you must inspire your sales team to embrace continuous learning and apply new skills in their daily interactions. But how do you ignite that initial excitement and maintain momentum over time? How do you build and support bold curiosity?

In this chapter, we'll explore practical strategies to generate enthusiasm, sustain motivation, and foster a culture of continuous learning within your sales team. We'll delve into real-world examples and provide actionable frameworks to help you design programs that not only educate but also engage and empower your sales professionals.

THE IMPORTANCE OF ENGAGEMENT IN SALES ENABLEMENT

Engagement is the bridge between knowledge and action. An engaged sales team is more likely to:

- **Adopt New Strategies:** Embrace and implement new techniques learned during training.

- **Improve Performance:** Translate learning into better sales outcomes.

- **Contribute Ideas:** Share feedback and insights that can enhance enablement programs.

STATISTIC: Companies with highly engaged employees outperform their competitors by 147% in earnings per share (Source: Gallup).

STRATEGIES TO GENERATE INITIAL EXCITEMENT

1. Clearly Communicate the Value Proposition

Before launching any enablement initiative, articulate the "why" behind it.

ACTION STEPS:

- ☐ **Connect to Personal Goals:** Show how the program will help reps achieve their targets and advance their careers.

- ☐ **Highlight Benefits:** Emphasize improvements in efficiency, earnings potential, and customer relationships.

- ☐ **Use Success Stories:** Share examples of how similar initiatives have led to tangible results.

EXAMPLE STATEMENT: "By mastering these new consultative selling techniques, you'll be able to close deals 30% faster, increasing your commissions and freeing up time for more opportunities."

2. Involve Sales Leaders and Influencers

Leverage the influence of respected individuals within the team.

Approach:

- **Leadership Endorsement:** Have managers and executives communicate their support for the program.

- **Peer Champions:** Identify top performers to advocate for the initiative and share their experiences.

  CASE STUDY: At Innovate Corp, involving top sales reps as program ambassadors increased initial training participation by 50%.

3. Create a Compelling Launch Event

Kick off the program with an engaging event.

Ideas:

- **Interactive Workshops:** Host sessions that involve games, simulations, or competitions.

- **Guest Speakers:** Invite industry experts to share insights and inspire the team.

- **Teasers and Promotions:** Use emails, videos, or posters to build anticipation.

SUSTAINING MOTIVATION OVER TIME

1. Implement Coaching Cohorts

Small groups that support each other's learning journey.

Benefits:

- **Accountability:** Peers hold each other responsible for applying new skills.

- **Collaboration:** Sharing challenges and solutions fosters collective growth.

- **Support:** Cohorts provide a safe space to discuss setbacks and celebrate successes.

How to Form Cohorts:

- **Group by Common Goals:** Assemble reps with similar objectives or challenges.

- **Assign a Coach:** Include a senior rep or manager to guide the group.

Once you have sparked initial enthusiasm and created structures to sustain it, the next challenge is embedding these practices deeply within your organization's DNA. This is where building a culture of continuous learning comes into play.

2. Encourage Peer-to-Peer Learning

Facilitate knowledge sharing among team members.

Methods:

- **Lunch and Learn Sessions:** Casual meetings where reps present on topics of expertise.

- **Internal Forums or Communities:** Online platforms for asking questions and sharing resources.

- **Shadowing Opportunities:** Allow reps to observe top performers in action.

  TIP: Recognize and reward contributions to peer learning to encourage participation.

3. Provide Ongoing Recognition and Rewards

Acknowledge efforts and achievements to maintain enthusiasm. By publicly celebrating achievements, you reinforce desired behaviors, making it easier to replicate success across the entire team.

Strategies:

- **Public Recognition:** Celebrate successes in team meetings or company newsletters.

- **Incentive Programs:** Offer bonuses, gifts, or additional opportunities for those who excel.

- **Progress Tracking:** Use leaderboards or dashboards to display achievements.

- **Addressing Potential Objections:** Consider how best to handle reps who don't want to participate, or fear judgement from their peers. This is why top-down leadership engagement is so important when launching the program. Also, addressing these concerns head-on in a supportive, and open conversation tends to have positive impact on engagement.

STATISTIC: Recognized employees are 2.7 times more likely to be highly engaged (Source: Deloitte).

BUILDING A CULTURE OF CONTINUOUS LEARNING

1. Integrate Learning into Daily Routines

Make learning a natural part of the workday.

Tactics:

- **Microlearning Moments:** Share quick tips or insights during daily huddles.

- **Learning Breaks:** Allocate time each week for reps to focus on development.

- **Accessible Resources:** Provide easy access to training materials through mobile apps or intranet portals.

2. Set Expectations and Goals

Establish clear expectations for ongoing development.

ACTION STEPS:

- ☐ **Personal Development Plans:** Work with reps to set individual learning objectives.

☐ **Regular Check-ins:** Incorporate progress discussions into one-on-one meetings.

☐ **Performance Metrics:** Tie learning outcomes to performance evaluations.

3. Foster an Environment of Curiosity

Encourage questions and exploration.

Approach:

- **Open Forums:** Create spaces where reps can ask questions without judgment.

- **Innovation Challenges:** Invite reps to develop and present new ideas or strategies.

- **Leadership Modeling:** Have leaders demonstrate their own commitment to learning.

"An investment in knowledge pays the best interest."
Benjamin Franklin

REAL-WORLD EXAMPLE: CULTIVATING ENGAGEMENT AT PEAK SALES

COMPANY: Peak Sales Solutions

CHALLENGE: Low engagement in training programs led to inconsistent application of sales methodologies.

Solution:

1. *Launched with Impact:* Organized a dynamic kickoff event featuring a motivational speaker and interactive sessions.

2. *Created Coaching Cohorts:* Formed groups led by high-performing reps to foster peer learning.

3. *Implemented Recognition Programs:* Introduced monthly awards for learning milestones and sales achievements.

4. *Integrated Learning Tools:* Adopted a mobile-friendly LMS for accessible, on-the-go training.

Results:

- **Increased Training Completion Rates:** From 60% to 90% within six months.

- **Improved Sales Performance:** Overall sales increased by 25% year-over-year.

- **Enhanced Team Morale:** Employee satisfaction scores improved by 30%.

ACTIONABLE FRAMEWORK: THE EMPOWER MODEL FOR ENGAGEMENT

Use this framework to design and sustain engaging sales enablement programs.

1. *Engage Early:* Generate excitement from the outset.

2. *Make It Relevant:* Ensure content aligns with reps' needs and goals.

3. ***Provide Support:*** Offer coaching and resources to facilitate learning.

4. ***Open Communication:*** Encourage feedback and dialogue.

5. ***Win Together:*** Celebrate individual and team successes.

6. ***Evolve Continuously:*** Adapt programs based on feedback and changing needs.

7. ***Reinforce Learning:*** Use assessments and real-world application to solidify skills.

LEVERAGING ONLINE COMMUNITIES TO ENHANCE ENGAGEMENT

In today's interconnected business environment, building an online community is a powerful strategy to foster engagement, collaboration, and continuous learning among your sales team. An online community provides a centralized space where team members can share insights, ask questions, and support each other's growth, transcending geographical boundaries and time zones.

The Power of Community in Sales Enablement

Benefits of Building an Online Community:

- **Knowledge Sharing:** Facilitates the exchange of best practices, tips, and resources.

- **Collaboration:** Encourages teamwork and collective problem-solving.

- **Peer Support:** Provides a platform for reps to motivate and learn from each other.

- **Continuous Engagement:** Keeps the team connected between formal training sessions.

  STATISTIC: Organizations that leverage online communities for learning see a 35% increase in knowledge retention among employees (Source: Brandon Hall Group).

Leveraging Circle.so for Community Building

To effectively create and manage an online community, utilizing the right platform is crucial. Circle.so is an all-in-one community platform that seamlessly integrates discussions, content sharing, and networking features, making it an excellent choice for sales enablement initiatives.

Features of Circle.so:

- **Customizable Spaces:** Create dedicated channels or groups for different topics, teams, or projects.

- **Integrated Content Sharing:** Easily share resources like training materials, videos, and articles.

- **Engagement Tools:** Use polls, events, and notifications to keep members active and informed.

- **Analytics:** Monitor community engagement and participation metrics to inform your strategies.

- **Integration Capabilities:** Connect with other tools in your tech stack for a cohesive experience.

  SHOUTOUT TO JORDAN GODBEY: A special acknowledgment to Jordan Godbey, whose support and expertise have been instrumental in helping organizations build thriving online communities. Jordan's insights into community engagement strategies have greatly enhanced our ability to connect and empower our sales teams. Noelle Russell and her amazingly generous knowledge sharing on her "I ♥ AI Community."

Best Practices for Building an Online Sales Community

Define the Community's Purpose:

- **Clarify Objectives:** Determine what you want to achieve; knowledge sharing, onboarding support, product updates, etc.

- **Set Guidelines:** Establish community norms to foster respectful and productive interactions.

Encourage Active Participation

- **Leadership Involvement:** Have managers and leaders participate to demonstrate commitment.

- **Recognition:** Acknowledge and reward valuable contributions from members.

- **Regular Engagement:** Post discussion prompts, host virtual events, or share weekly tips.

Foster Inclusivity and Accessibility

- **Ensure Accessibility:** Make the community easy to access and navigate for all team members.

- **Promote Diverse Voices:** Encourage participation from members across different regions and roles.

- **Provide Support:** Offer guidance on how to use the platform effectively.

Integrate with Sales Enablement Programs

- **Align Content:** Share resources and discussions related to ongoing training initiatives.

- **Integrate Feedback Mechanisms:** Use the community to gather input on enablement programs and identify areas for improvement.

- **Peer Learning:** Facilitate mentorship programs and group learning activities within the community.

Measuring Community Impact

To ensure your online community is delivering value, track engagement and impact:

- **Engagement Metrics:** Monitor active users, post frequency, and interaction levels.

- **Knowledge Sharing:** Assess the quality and usefulness of shared content.

- **Performance Correlation:** Analyze how community participation relates to sales performance metrics.

- **Feedback Surveys:** Regularly solicit feedback from members on their community experience.

Real-World Example: Building a Vibrant Community with Circle.so

At a startup, we successfully developed and executed an online community using Circle.so, branding it and growing it to nearly 1,000 members in less than three months. Through this platform, we:

- **Developed Courses:** Created and shared valuable training courses, including the Power Prompting course.

- **Engaged Members:** Fostered strong community engagement by cultivating relationships with thought leaders, including Erin Reddick, founder of ChatBlackGPT (addressing bias in generative AI outputs), and Professor Jules White, who leverages generative AI for creative augmentation.

- **Enhanced Learning:** Delivered weekly technical "How To" workshop sessions, collaborating with the Head of Design to create completion certificates.

- **Acknowledgment:** The support from Circle.so and insights from professionals like Jordan Godbey were instrumental in building and nurturing this thriving community.

Harnessing the Power of Online Communities

Integrating an online community into your sales enablement strategy can significantly enhance engagement and foster a culture of continuous learning. By leveraging platforms like Circle.so and drawing on the expertise of community professionals such as Jordan Godbey, you can create a dynamic space that empowers your sales team to connect, collaborate, and excel.

Key Takeaways:

- **Community Enhances Engagement:** An online community provides a platform for ongoing interaction and support among sales reps.

- **Leverage the Right Tools:** Platforms like Circle.so offer features tailored to building and managing effective communities.

- **Best Practices Matter:** Successful communities require clear objectives, active participation, inclusivity, and alignment with broader enablement programs.

- **Measure Impact:** Regularly assess community engagement and its correlation with sales performance to ensure continued value.

CALL TO ACTION:

☐ Explore Community Platforms: Consider how an online community could benefit your sales team and investigate platforms like Circle.so.

☐ Engage with Experts: Reach out to professionals like Jordan Godbey for insights on building and managing your community.

☐ Start Building: Define your community's purpose and begin fostering connections among your sales team.

CONCLUSION: EMPOWERING YOUR SALES TEAM FOR SUCCESS

Driving engagement and motivation in sales enablement is an on-going journey. By creating programs that resonate with your sales team, fostering a supportive learning environment, and recognizing their efforts, you empower your reps to achieve greater success.

Key Takeaways:

- **Start Strong:** Generate initial excitement with clear communication and impactful launches.

- **Sustain Momentum:** Use coaching, peer learning, and recognition to keep motivation high.

- **Cultivate a Learning Culture:** Integrate development into daily routines and organizational values.

Are you ready to energize your sales team and unlock their full potential?

In the next chapter, we'll explore how to measure the impact of your sales enablement initiatives and effectively communicate success to stakeholders.

CHAPTER SUMMARY

⇒ Engagement Importance: Vital for translating knowledge into action.

⇒ Generating Excitement: Communicate value, involve leaders, create impactful launches.

⇒ Sustaining Motivation: Coaching cohorts, peer learning, recognition programs.

⇒ Continuous Learning Culture: Integrate learning, set goals, foster curiosity.

⇒ Real-World Example: Peak Sales Solutions' successful engagement strategies.

⇒ SEID: Framework for designing engaging sustainable inclusive programs.

⇒ Leveraging Online Communities: Jasper.ai's community, Noelle Russell's community, Brendon Bruchard's community and more!

CALL TO ACTION

- ☐ Assess Engagement Levels: Evaluate current motivation and participation in your programs.
- ☐ Implement One New Strategy: Choose a tactic from this chapter to boost engagement.
- ☐ Gather Feedback: Solicit input from your sales team on what motivates them.

By prioritizing engagement and motivation, you're not just enhancing your sales enablement programs—you're investing in the growth and satisfaction of your sales team, leading to better performance and a stronger organization.

FREQUENTLY ASKED QUESTIONS
Driving Engagement and Motivation in Sales Enablement

1. **How can I increase engagement and motivation among my sales team for enablement initiatives?**

   Strategies include involving sales reps in program development, aligning training with their personal goals, recognizing and rewarding participation, fostering a culture of continuous learning, and leveraging engaging content and interactive platforms. Focus on strengths and work on the gaps. Continuously promote their successes! Celebrate every win and acknowledge each share.

2. **What role does an online community play in sales enablement?**

An online community facilitates knowledge sharing, peer support, collaboration, and continuous engagement among sales reps. It provides a centralized space for discussions, resources, and fostering a sense of belonging. In this book I have recommended Circle.so as a great online community environment.

3. **How do I effectively leverage platforms like Circle.so for building an online community?**

Use Circle.so to create customizable spaces for different topics, share content, host events, and encourage interaction using "challenges" and gamifying the experience. Engage members through regular updates, discussions, and by highlighting contributions. Ensure whatever platform is being used is user-friendly and aligns with your community's (your target audience's) needs.

4. **What are some best practices for maintaining long term engagement in sales enablement programs?**

Regularly update content, solicit feedback, adapt to changing needs, recognize achievements, provide opportunities for growth, and keep communication open and transparent. You need to stay in sync with the product and company roadmap and know what is happening in the field. Are there specific ongoing constraints you need to be aware of, has there been a shift in specific regions? Build strong relationships with the teams you are working enabling clear and frequent communication.

Ultimately, engagement and motivation aren't just feel-good strategies, they are the fuel that propels your sales team to deliver outstanding results and drive measurable business growth.

CHAPTER 6

MEASURING IMPACT AND COMMUNICATING SUCCESS

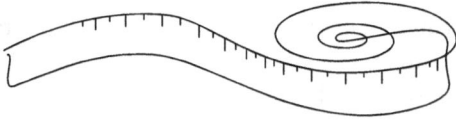

Implementing sales enablement initiatives is a significant investment, and like any investment, it demands a clear return. To justify continued support and resources, you must demonstrate how these programs contribute to the organization's bottom line. Measuring impact isn't just about numbers; it's about telling a compelling story that connects your efforts to tangible business outcomes.

In this chapter, we'll delve into effective strategies for measuring the impact of your sales enablement initiatives. We'll discuss key performance indicators (KPIs), data collection methods, and how to communicate results to stakeholders in a way that underscores the value of your programs. With your data in hand, the next critical step is turning numbers into narratives. By communicating results effectively, you ensure that your efforts gain the recognition and support they deserve.

Real-world examples and actionable frameworks will equip you with the tools needed to showcase success and drive continuous improvement.

THE IMPORTANCE OF MEASUREMENT IN SALES ENABLEMENT

Metrics and ROI are the cornerstone of ensuring your programs are not just operational but impactful. These measurements provide clarity on performance, help refine strategies, and secure continued investment.

One way ROI can be calculated is by dividing the net profit generated by the program by the total cost of the program. Understanding this ratio helps you quickly convey financial impact.

There can be specific key metrics in your organization. These matter, so be sure you are aware and tracking the targeted key metrics. Confirm you have viewing access to know the landscape of your team and know what matters most to them.

Measurement provides the evidence needed to:

- **Validate Efforts:** Prove that initiatives are yielding desired results.

- **Inform Decisions:** Use data to refine strategies and allocate resources effectively.

- **Gain Stakeholder Buy-In:** Secure ongoing support from leadership and other departments.

  STATISTIC: Organizations that leverage data-driven sales enablement see 19% faster revenue growth (Source: McKinsey & Company).

Identifying Key Performance Indicators (KPIs)

Select metrics that align with your business goals and provide meaningful insights.

Performance Metrics

WHY IT MATTERS: Directly reflects the effectiveness of sales strategies and skills.

Examples:

- **Win Rate:** Percentage of closed deals compared to total opportunities.

- **Quota Attainment:** Proportion of sales reps meeting or exceeding targets.

- **Average Deal Size:** Monetary value of deals closed.

Efficiency Metrics

WHY IT MATTERS: Indicates how enablement initiatives streamline processes.

Examples:

- **Time-to-Productivity:** Time it takes new reps to reach full performance levels.

- **Sales Cycle Length:** Duration from initial contact to deal closure.

- **Lead Conversion Rate:** Percentage of leads converted into customers.

Engagement Metrics

WHY IT MATTERS: Reflects the adoption and perceived value of enablement efforts.

Examples:

- **Training Completion Rates:** Percentage of reps completing training programs.

- **Content Utilization:** Frequency and manner in which sales materials are used.

- **Feedback Scores:** Satisfaction ratings from reps on training and resources.

Behavioral Metrics

WHY IT MATTERS: Shows how training translates into real-world behavior.

Examples:

- **Adoption of Best Practices:** Extent to which reps use recommended approaches.

- **Customer Satisfaction Scores:** Feedback from clients on sales interactions.

- **Cross-Selling and Upselling Rates:** Instances of reps expanding customer purchases.

ROI Calculation

WHY IT MATTERS: Ultimately, ROI and measurements ensures that your enablement initiatives remain dynamic, strategic, and closely tied to the broader objectives of the business.

Examples:

- **Direct Revenue Attribution:** Tie specific deals or revenue growth directly to enablement efforts.

- **Cost-to-Revenue Ratio:** Compare the cost of sales enablement programs to revenue gains.

DATA COLLECTION AND ANALYSIS METHODS

Utilize Technology Platforms

Leverage tools that automatically track and report data.

Tools:

- **CRM Systems:** Capture sales activities and outcomes.

- **LMS Analytics:** Monitor training engagement and progress.

- **Sales Enablement Platforms:** Track content usage and effectiveness.

Conduct Surveys and Assessments

Gather qualitative data directly from participants.

Approach:

- **Post-Training Surveys:** Collect feedback on content relevance and delivery.

- **Self-Assessments:** Allow reps to evaluate their confidence and skill levels.

- **Customer Feedback:** Use Net Promoter Score (NPS) or similar metrics.

Hold Performance Reviews

Regular check-ins to discuss progress and challenges.

Benefits:

- **Identify Trends:** Spot patterns in performance data.

- **Personalize Support:** Tailor coaching to individual needs.

- **Adjust Goals:** Realign objectives based on findings.

Once you've gathered relevant data, the next challenge is translating those insights into compelling messages that resonate with stakeholders.

COMMUNICATING SUCCESS TO STAKEHOLDERS

Know Your Audience

Tailor your message to the interests and priorities of different stakeholders.

Stakeholder Groups:

- **Executive Leadership:** Focus on high-level impact and ROI.

- **Sales Managers:** Highlight team performance and coaching opportunities.

- **Cross-Functional Teams:** Emphasize collaboration benefits and shared goals.

Tell a Compelling Story

Use data to craft a narrative that connects your initiatives to business outcomes.

Components:

- **Situation:** Describe the challenges faced before the initiative.

- **Action:** Outline the steps taken to address them.

- **Result:** Present the tangible outcomes achieved.

> **EXAMPLE STATEMENT:** "After implementing our new onboarding program, new hires reached full productivity 30% faster, contributing to a $2 million increase in quarterly revenue."

Use Visual Aids

Enhance understanding and retention with graphics.

Tools:

- **Dashboards:** Interactive displays of real-time data.

- **Infographics:** Visual summaries of key metrics and results.

- **Charts and Graphs:** Illustrate trends and comparisons.

Be Transparent and Objective

Present both successes and areas for improvement.

Approach:

- **Acknowledge Challenges:** Discuss obstacles encountered and how they're being addressed.

- **Provide Context:** Explain factors that may have influenced results.

- **Offer Recommendations:** Suggest next steps based on data insights. Engage with collaborative Generative AI tools to enhance your recommendations and reporting dashboards.

REAL-WORLD EXAMPLE: DEMONSTRATING IMPACT AT TECHSOLUTIONS

COMPANY: TechSolutions Inc.

CHALLENGE: Leadership was skeptical about the ROI of sales enablement programs.

Solution:

- **Defined Clear KPIs:** Aligned metrics with company goals, focusing on win rates and time-to-productivity.

- **Implemented Robust Data Tracking:** Leveraged CRM and LMS tools for accurate data collection.

- **Crafted Impact Reports:** Created quarterly presentations showcasing results with visual aids.

- **Engaged Stakeholders:** Held meetings with executives and managers to discuss findings and gather feedback.

Results:

- **Win Rate Increase:** Improved by 15% within six months.

- **Reduced Onboarding Time:** New reps reached productivity two weeks sooner.

- **Secured Increased Funding:** Leadership approved additional resources for program expansion.

ACTIONABLE FRAMEWORK: THE MEASURE APPROACH

Utilize this framework to effectively measure and communicate impact.

1. *Map Objectives:* Align KPIs with business goals.

2. *Engage Stakeholders:* Involve key parties in defining success metrics.

3. *Aggregate Data:* Collect information from multiple sources for a comprehensive view.

4. *Synthesize Findings:* Analyze data to extract meaningful insights.

5. *Utilize Visuals:* Present data in an accessible and engaging format.

6. *Report Regularly:* Maintain consistent communication with stakeholders.

7. *Evaluate and Iterate:* Use findings to refine programs and strategies.

After demonstrating value and earning stakeholder support, it's time to leverage these insights for ongoing refinement and growth.

DRIVING CONTINUOUS IMPROVEMENT

Analyze Data for Insights

Look beyond surface-level metrics.

Considerations:

- **Identify Root Causes:** Understand why certain results occurred.

- **Segment Data:** Break down metrics by team, region, or product line.

- **Benchmark:** Compare performance against industry standards or past results.

Solicit Feedback

Engage with your sales team and stakeholders.

Methods:

- **Focus Groups:** Gather in-depth insights from select participants.

- **Suggestion Boxes:** Provide anonymous channels for input.

- **Advisory Committees:** Form groups to guide program development.

Implement Changes and Monitor Effects

Act on findings and track the impact of adjustments.

Approach:

- **Pilot Programs:** Test changes on a small scale before full rollout.

- **Set Review Dates:** Schedule future evaluations to assess effectiveness.

- **Document Learnings:** Keep records of what works and what doesn't.

CONCLUSION: SHOWCASING THE VALUE OF SALES ENABLEMENT

Measuring and communicating the impact of your sales enablement initiatives is crucial for demonstrating value and securing ongoing support. By focusing on relevant KPIs, utilizing effective data collection methods, and presenting your findings compellingly, you can highlight the significant contributions these programs make to organizational success.

Key Takeaways:

- **Align Metrics with Goals:** Ensure you're measuring what matters most to your organization.

- **Tell a Story with Data:** Use narratives and visuals to make data meaningful.

- **Drive Improvement:** Use insights gained to refine and enhance your programs.

Ready to showcase the impact of your sales enablement efforts and drive even greater success?

In the next chapter, we'll explore how to scale your sales enablement programs across the organization, ensuring consistency and sustained impact as your business grows.

CHAPTER SUMMARY

⇒ Measurement Importance: Validating efforts, informing decisions, gaining buy-in.

⇒ Key KPIs: Performance, efficiency, engagement, behavioral metrics.

⇒ Data Collection: Technology tools, surveys, performance reviews.

⇒ Communicating Success: Know your audience, tell a compelling story, use visuals.

⇒ Continuous Improvement: Analyze data, solicit feedback, implement changes.

⇒ Real-World Example: TechSolutions Inc.'s effective impact measurement.

CALL TO ACTION

☐ Define Your KPIs: Select metrics that align with your organization's objectives.

☐ Set Up Data Tracking: Ensure you have systems in place to collect necessary data.

☐ Prepare Your First Impact Report: Compile your findings and plan how to present them to stakeholders.

By effectively measuring and communicating the success of your sales enablement initiatives, you not only demonstrate their value but also pave the way for continuous growth and improvement within your organization.

Interactive Reflective Questions

- How aligned are your sales enablement KPIs with business goals?

- What specific metrics are you tracking to measure the success of your sales enablement initiatives?

- How do you gather feedback from your sales teams to continuously improve your enablement programs?

- How can you integrate data from different sources to measure the complete impact of your enablement efforts?

FREQUENTLY ASKED QUESTIONS
Measuring Impact and Communicating Success

1. **What metrics are essential for measuring sales enablement success?**

   Essential metrics include win rates, quota attainment, time-to-productivity, and content utilization. Align these with the organization's objectives to measure both qualitative and quantitative success.

2. **What are the most important metrics to track for sales enablement effectiveness?**

   Align with sales leadership to define the real key metrics for your teams. Key metrics can include sales performance indicators (e.g., quota attainment, win rates), training completion and effectiveness, content utilization rates, time-to-productivity, and ROI of enablement initiatives.

3. **How do I collect and analyze data to measure impact?**

   Use analytics tools integrated with your LMS, CRM, and other platforms to collect data. Regularly analyze this data to identify trends, areas for improvement, and correlations between enablement activities and sales outcomes. Know how your sales leadership views their team's data. Leverage similar dashboards and try to find correlation between training completions and changes in target attainments.

4. **How can I effectively communicate the success of sales enablement programs to stakeholders?**

   Use clear, concise reports focusing on key metrics and ROI. Tailor communication to your audience by highlighting the most relevant data. Executives may prefer high-level summaries, while managers might appreciate more detailed insights. Use visual aids like charts and graphs to illustrate points. Leverage the dashboards the team leadership is already using to enhance both your credibility and ease absorption of information. For example, if they are using Salesforce dashboards, it would be beneficial for you to use the same dashboards with your data points.

5. **What tools should I use to track and analyze sales enablement impact?**

Use CRM systems (like Salesforce), LMS tools, and reporting platforms like Tableau or Power BI. Integrating these tools ensures comprehensive data collection. Make sure to know what the tools are being used by your leadership and are known to your sales teams. If there are tools and they are being used, is this a leadership issue? Is it a training issue. Investigate and resolve!

6. **What should I do if the data shows that my sales enablement programs are not having the desired impact?**

Investigate the underlying causes by gathering feedback, reviewing program content and delivery methods, and reassessing alignment with business goals. Use these insights to adjust and improve your programs. This is the time to pivot and improve your content. Iterating on content and delivery methods is essential for success. Don't wait until the program completes, find access points of gathering data while the program is ongoing and pivot and iterate immediately if the data is showing a need. Your responsiveness will increase your authority on training content and will be appreciated by both participants and leadership. This is why piloting content with a small, engaged group is essential, and why staying on top of your data is so important.

CHAPTER 7

SCALING SALES ENABLEMENT ACROSS THE ORGANIZATION

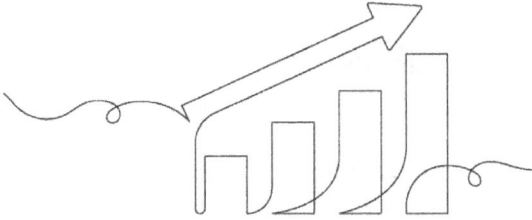

As your sales enablement initiatives begin to yield positive results, the next challenge is scaling these programs across your entire organization. Scaling isn't just about replicating what works; it's about adapting your strategies to fit different teams, regions, and market dynamics while maintaining consistency and impact. Done right, scaling can amplify your success and establish sales enablement as a core driver of business growth.

In this chapter, we'll explore practical steps and frameworks for effectively scaling your sales enablement efforts. We'll delve into real-world examples, discuss common challenges, and provide actionable insights to help you expand your programs seamlessly. By the end, you'll be equipped with the knowledge to extend your enablement initiatives organization-wide, ensuring sustained success and a competitive edge in the marketplace.

THE IMPORTANCE OF SCALING SALES ENABLEMENT

Scaling sales enablement is crucial for:

- **Consistent Performance:** Ensuring all teams have access to the same resources and training for uniform excellence.

- **Operational Efficiency:** Streamlining processes to reduce duplication of efforts across departments.

- **Strategic Alignment:** Aligning sales strategies with overarching business goals at every level.

- **Competitive Advantage:** Leveraging collective insights and best practices to stay ahead in the market.

> **STATISTIC:** Organizations that effectively scale their sales enablement programs see a 10% increase in sales quota attainment across all teams (Source: Sales Enablement Collective).

CHALLENGES IN SCALING SALES ENABLEMENT

Before diving into strategies, it's important to recognize common obstacles:

Diverse Needs across Teams

Different teams may have varied:

- **Skill Levels:** New hires vs. seasoned professionals.

- **Market Focus:** Enterprise clients vs. small businesses.

- **Cultural Contexts:** Regional differences in communication styles and business practices.

Resource Constraints

- **Limited Budgets:** Allocating funds across multiple departments.

- **Technology Gaps:** Inconsistent access to tools and platforms.

- **Staffing Limitations:** Insufficient personnel to manage expanded programs.

Resistance to Change

- **Adoption Hurdles:** Hesitance from teams comfortable with existing processes.

- **Communication Breakdowns:** Misalignment between departments leading to confusion.

- **Cultural Barriers:** Differing organizational cultures impeding standardization.

Having recognized these common challenges, let's explore strategies that will help you navigate them successfully as you scale.

STRATEGIES FOR EFFECTIVE SCALING

To effectively scale, consider these essential strategies that build on each other, starting with a strong foundation, then customizing for local contexts, and finally leveraging the right tools and governance structures. This topic is emphasized providing support to an important area of growth for many of these programs.

Start with a Strong Foundation

Ensure your core sales enablement program is robust before scaling.

Action Steps:

- **Document Processes:** Create detailed guides and playbooks.

- **Establish Best Practices:** Identify what works and why.

- **Secure Leadership Buy-In:** Gain support from executives to champion the scaling effort. For example, ensure a senior leader regularly communicates updates on scaling efforts during company-wide meetings, reinforcing the importance of the initiative.

  EXAMPLE: A leading software company standardized their onboarding process, reducing new hire ramp-up time by 40% before rolling it out globally.

Customize While Maintaining Consistency

Balance standardization with necessary customization.

Approach:

- **Core Curriculum:** Maintain a universal foundation of training content.

- **Localized Adaptations:** Modify materials to reflect regional market nuances and cultural differences.

- **Flexible Frameworks:** Provide templates that teams can tailor to their needs.

> **CASE STUDY:** Global Tech Inc. implemented a global sales training program with localized case studies and role-plays relevant to each region, increasing engagement by 35%.

Leverage Technology for Scalability

Utilize tools that support expansion. When selecting an LMS, consider factors like multilingual support, mobile accessibility, ease of administration and reporting capabilities. Ease of integration with your existing CRM is vital to ensure a smooth global rollout.

Tools:

- **Learning Management Systems (LMS):** Utilize platforms like Cornerstone or Docebo for distributing content globally.

- **Cloud-Based Repositories:** Centralized access to resources via platforms like Google Drive or SharePoint.

- **Collaboration Software:** Tools like Slack or Microsoft Teams for cross-team communication.

Benefits:

- **Accessibility:** Ensure all teams can access the same resources.

- **Consistency:** Maintain up-to-date content across the organization.

- **Efficiency:** Automate processes to reduce manual workload.

Establish a Governance Structure

Create a framework to manage and oversee the scaling process.

Components:

- **Steering Committee:** A group of stakeholders from different departments and regions to guide decisions.

- **Roles and Responsibilities:** Clearly defined tasks for team members involved in enablement.

- **Policies and Guidelines:** Standard operating procedures to ensure consistency.

  TIP: Regular meetings and updates help keep everyone aligned and informed.

Foster Cross-Functional Collaboration

Scaling is a team effort that requires input from multiple departments.

Strategies:

- **Regular Alignment Meetings:** Schedule sessions with sales, marketing, product, and customer success teams.

- **Shared Goals and KPIs:** Develop common objectives to encourage collaboration.

- **Feedback Mechanisms:** Create channels for continuous input and suggestions.

  EXAMPLE: A multinational corporation increased its sales by 20% after integrating feedback loops between sales and product teams during the scaling process.

Invest in Training and Support

Provide ongoing education to facilitate adoption.

Actions:

- **Train-the-Trainer Programs:** Equip regional leaders to deliver training effectively.

- **Resource Libraries:** Offer self-service materials for continuous learning.

- **Help Desks and Support Teams:** Provide assistance for technical or procedural questions.

Monitor, Measure, and Adjust

Use data to inform decisions and refine strategies.

Metrics to Track:

- **Adoption Rates:** Percentage of teams using the new programs.

- **Performance Metrics:** Sales figures, win rates, customer satisfaction scores.

- **Feedback Scores:** Surveys and assessments from participants.

Iterative Process:

- **Analyze Data:** Identify trends and areas needing improvement.

- **Adjust Strategies:** Refine programs based on insights.

- **Communicate Changes:** Keep all stakeholders informed about updates.

REAL-WORLD EXAMPLE: SCALING SUCCESS AT ELITE SALES CORP

COMPANY: Elite Sales Corp, a global manufacturing firm.

CHALLENGE: Disparate sales processes across regions led to inconsistent performance and messaging.

Elite Sales Corp, a global manufacturing firm struggling with fragmented regional approaches, embarked on a scaling initiative to unify their sales messaging and improve global consistency.

Solution:

1. *Assessment:* Conducted a global audit to understand regional needs and challenges.

2. *Standardization:* Developed a core sales enablement program with input from regional leaders.

3. *Localization:* Adapted training materials to reflect local markets, languages, and cultural nuances.

4. *Technology Implementation:* Deployed a unified LMS accessible worldwide, integrated with their CRM.

5. *Governance Structure:* Established a global sales enablement council with representatives from each region.

6. *Training:* Initiated train-the-trainer workshops to empower local managers.

7. **Continuous Improvement:** Set up regular review cycles to assess effectiveness and make adjustments.

Results:

- **Consistent Messaging:** Unified brand and product messaging across all markets.

- **Performance Boost:** Achieved a 15% increase in global sales revenue within a year.

- **Enhanced Collaboration:** Improved communication and knowledge sharing between regions.

ACTIONABLE FRAMEWORK: THE SCALE MODEL FOR EXPANSION

Utilize this framework to guide your scaling efforts.

1. **Standardize Core Elements:** Define essential training and resources that apply universally.

2. **Customize for Local Needs:** Adapt materials to address regional differences.

3. **Align Stakeholders:** Engage leaders and teams across departments and regions.

4. **Leverage Technology:** Use scalable tools for training, communication, and resource management.

5. **Evaluate and Evolve:** Monitor progress and refine strategies based on data and feedback.

OVERCOMING COMMON OBSTACLES

Below are some of the previously identified challenges, paired with strategies to overcome them:

Resistance to Change

Solution:

- **Communicate Benefits:** Clearly articulate how the scaled program will improve outcomes.

- **Involve Teams Early:** Engage teams in the planning process to foster ownership.

- **Provide Support:** Offer training and resources to ease the transition. Do not minimize the importance of change management!

Inconsistent Adoption

Solution:

- **Set Clear Expectations:** Define what is required and by when.

- **Monitor Adoption Rates:** Use metrics to identify lagging areas.

- **Recognize and Reward:** Acknowledge teams that successfully implement the programs.

Cultural and Language Barriers

Solution:

- **Local Expertise:** Utilize local staff to adapt content appropriately.

- **Multilingual Materials:** Translate resources to accommodate different languages.

- **Cultural Sensitivity Training:** Educate teams on cultural nuances.

CONCLUSION: SCALING FOR SUSTAINABLE SUCCESS

Scaling your sales enablement programs is a strategic move that can significantly enhance your organization's performance and competitiveness. By thoughtfully expanding your initiatives, you ensure that all teams are equipped with the tools, knowledge, and support they need to excel.

Key Takeaways:

- **Plan Strategically:** A deliberate approach ensures smoother scaling.

- **Balance Consistency and Flexibility:** Standardize core elements while allowing for local adaptations.

- **Engage and Empower:** Involve stakeholders at all levels to drive adoption.

- **Leverage Technology:** Utilize tools that facilitate scalability and efficiency.

- **Monitor and Adapt:** Use data-driven insights to continuously improve.

Are you prepared to scale your sales enablement efforts and unlock new levels of organizational success?

As we conclude this book, remember that sales enablement is a journey of continuous learning, adaptation, and growth. By applying the strategies and frameworks discussed, you're well on your way to building high-impact teams that drive remarkable business results.

CHAPTER SUMMARY

⇒ **IMPORTANCE OF SCALING:** Enhances consistency, efficiency, alignment, and competitive advantage.

⇒ **CHALLENGES:** Diverse team needs, resource constraints, resistance to change.

⇒ **EFFECTIVE STRATEGIES:**
- *Start with a strong foundation.*
- *Customize while maintaining consistency.*
- *Leverage technology.*
- *Establish governance.*
- *Foster cross-functional collaboration.*
- *Invest in training and support.*
- *Monitor, measure, and adjust.*

Remember that scaling is iterative. Regularly revisit your strategies, update content as markets evolve, and remain open to feedback from frontline sales teams.

⇒ **REAL-WORLD EXAMPLE:** Elite Sales Corp's successful scaling journey.

⇒ **SCALE MODEL:** Framework to guide scaling efforts.

➡ **OVERCOMING OBSTACLES:** Address resistance, adoption issues, cultural barriers.

CALL TO ACTION

☐ Assess Readiness: Evaluate your current programs and organizational readiness for scaling.

☐ Develop a Scaling Plan: Outline steps based on the SCALE model.

☐ Engage Stakeholders: Begin discussions with leaders and teams across the organization.

☐ Initiate Pilot Programs: Test scaling strategies in select regions or departments.

By thoughtfully scaling your sales enablement initiatives, you not only enhance the capabilities of your sales teams but also drive your organization toward greater cohesion and success in an increasingly competitive market.

FREQUENTLY ASKED QUESTIONS
Scaling Sales Enablement Across the Organization

1. **What are the key considerations when scaling sales enablement programs?**

   Consider consistency versus customization, resource allocation, technology infrastructure, cultural differences across regions, and maintaining quality while expanding reach.

2. **How do I balance the need for standardized programs with the need for regional customization?**

   Develop core content and frameworks that can be adapted to local contexts. Involve regional leaders in tailoring programs to meet specific needs while maintaining alignment with overall objectives.

3. **What governance structures should I establish to manage scaling effectively?**

   Implement clear policies, roles, and responsibilities. Establish a central sales enablement team with regional representatives. Use consistent communication channels and reporting mechanisms to maintain alignment.

4. **How can I ensure sustained engagement and effectiveness as programs scale?**

   Continue to involve sales reps at all levels, adapt to feedback, invest in ongoing training for enablement staff, and leverage technology to facilitate communication and collaboration across the organization.

CHAPTER 8

CHARTING THE PATH FORWARD IN SALES ENABLEMENT

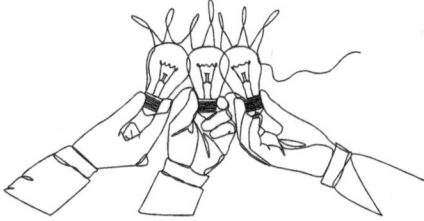

A s we conclude, it's important to reflect on the journey we've taken together. From understanding the critical role of sales enablement in today's business landscape to exploring strategies for scaling these initiatives across your organization, we've delved deep into the elements that make sales enablement a transformative force.

KEY TAKEAWAYS

- **Strategic Alignment Is Essential:** A well-crafted sales enablement strategy must align with your organization's overarching business goals to drive measurable results.

- **Technology Is a Powerful Enabler:** Building an effective tech stack enhances efficiency, collaboration, and data-driven decision-making.

- **Engagement Fuels Success:** Actively engaging and motivating your sales team leads to better adoption of enablement initiatives and improved performance.

- **Measurement Validates Impact:** By establishing clear KPIs and regularly assessing your programs, you can demonstrate value and secure ongoing support.

- **Scaling Requires Adaptation and Consistency:** Expanding your sales enablement efforts across the organization involves balancing standardization with customization to meet diverse needs.

EMBRACING CONTINUOUS LEARNING AND INNOVATION

Sales enablement is not a one-time project but an ongoing process of learning, adapting, and innovating. The marketplace will continue to evolve, and so must our strategies. By fostering a culture of continuous improvement and staying attuned to emerging trends—such as the integration of generative AI—you position your organization to thrive amid change.

YOUR NEXT STEPS

- **Apply the Frameworks:** Utilize the models and strategies discussed to assess and enhance your current sales enablement initiatives.

- **Engage with the Community:** Connect with peers, join professional networks, and participate in discussions to share insights and learn from others. Consider building your own community on circle.so!

- **Invest in Development:** Prioritize the growth and learning of your sales team, recognizing that their success is the organization's success.

Remember, the journey toward sales enablement excellence is a collaborative effort. Together, we can build high-impact teams that drive remarkable business results.

FINAL THOUGHTS: EMPOWERING YOUR ORGANIZATION THROUGH SALES ENABLEMENT

Embarking on the journey of enhancing your sales enablement efforts is both challenging and rewarding. Remember, the key to success lies in continuous learning, adaptation, and collaboration. Utilize the frameworks, insights, and resources provided in this book to build programs that not only achieve your organizational goals but also empower your sales teams to reach their full potential.

Sales enablement is more than a function—it's a strategic imperative that empowers your entire organization. From building robust strategies and leveraging technology to engaging your sales team and measuring impact, each step contributes to a powerful engine driving business growth.

Reminder:

- **Continuous Improvement:** Always seek ways to refine and enhance your programs.

- **Adaptability:** Stay responsive to market changes and organizational needs.

- **Collaboration:** Foster a culture where knowledge sharing and teamwork are valued.

The Joy of Sales Enablement: Transforming Teams for Greater Success

Sales enablement is more than a strategy, it's a journey of transformation, growth, and success. There's a unique joy in witnessing sales reps, and teams, evolve, from being uncertain about their approach to confidently aligning their skills with the broader company goals. At its core, sales enablement is about guiding teams to unlock their potential, achieve greater alignment, and become more effective contributors to the organization's vision.

Imagine a team at the beginning of the enablement journey. Sales reps may be focused solely on closing their own deals, not fully understanding how to connect their tactics with the company's strategy. Through sales enablement, we can help them become consultative sellers, professionals who understand their customers' pain points, offer valuable insights, and genuinely contribute to the success of their clients. The joy comes from watching them grow in both competence and confidence, stepping into the role of trusted advisors.

Another rewarding aspect of sales enablement is taking a team from inconsistent use of their sales workflow to global alignment. Initially, reps might be selling in different ways, depending on their region or previous experiences. With effective enablement, they learn to integrate the sales process globally, adopting consistent best practices leading to more consistent results across markets. This transformation not only drives measurable business outcomes, but it also creates a sense of unity and shared purpose within the sales team.

Whether the goal is becoming more consultative sellers, creating consistency across global teams, or fostering specific alignment with company objectives, sales enablement professionals have the unique opportunity to drive meaningful change. There's a deep sense of fulfillment that comes with seeing sales reps transform, not just in how they sell, but in how they think, how they engage with clients, and how they contribute to the organization's mission. This can also impact their self-perception, taking a sales rep from just doing the job, to feel empowered, and grow into engaged leadership.

The real magic of sales enablement lies in these transformations. It's not just about the numbers, it's about the people, the mindset shifts, and the incredible growth that happens when individuals and teams fully embrace the enablement journey. Witnessing these moments is what makes sales enablement such a rewarding endeavor. We aren't just enabling sales, we're nurturing growth, fostering excellence, and helping our teams realize the joy of achieving aligned, consistent, and impactful success.

Your journey doesn't end here. Use the insights and frameworks provided to propel your sales enablement efforts forward, creating high-impact teams and achieving remarkable results. Here's to your success in building and scaling sales enablement programs that make a lasting impact.

Thank you for investing your time in this book. I look forward to hearing about your successes and learning experiences as you apply these strategies in your organization. If you or your team are interested in personalized guidance or a tailored roadmap, please consider reaching out. I'm here to help your organization achieve its unique sales enablement goals.

INTERACTIVE REFLECTIVE QUESTIONS

To deepen your understanding and facilitate the application of the concepts discussed, review additional interactive reflective questions for each chapter:

Chapter 1: The Critical Role of Sales Enablement in Today's Business Landscape

1. *Assessment:* How does your organization's current sales enablement approach align with the challenges of today's informed buyers and competitive markets?

2. *Reflection:* What are the biggest gaps in your sales team's ability to engage effectively with prospects and customers?

3. *Action:* What immediate steps can you take to begin addressing these gaps?

Chapter 2: Crafting a Sales Enablement Strategy for Measurable Results

1. *Alignment:* Are your sales enablement initiatives aligned with your company's strategic business goals? How can you improve this alignment?

2. *Stakeholder Engagement:* Who are the key stakeholders that need to be involved in developing your sales enablement strategy?

3. *Measurement:* What KPIs will you use to measure the success of your enablement programs?

Chapter 3: Building a Sales Enablement Tech Stack for Optimal Performance

1. *Inventory:* What tools are currently part of your sales tech stack? Are they effectively integrated?

2. *Needs Analysis:* Where are the bottlenecks or inefficiencies in your sales process that technology could address?

3. *Planning:* How will you prioritize the implementation of new tools without overwhelming your team?

Chapter 4: Bringing Your Sales Enablement Vision to Life

1. *Program Design:* How can you tailor your sales enablement programs to accommodate different learning styles within your team?

2. *Technology Integration:* What emerging technologies, such as AI or VR, could enhance your training programs?

3. *Inclusivity:* In what ways can you ensure your programs are inclusive and accessible to all team members?

Chapter 5: Driving Engagement and Motivation in Sales Enablement

1. *Motivation:* What strategies can you implement to generate excitement about new sales enablement initiatives?

2. *Sustainability:* How will you maintain engagement and motivation over time?

3. *Culture:* What steps can you take to foster a culture of continuous learning within your sales team?

Chapter 6: Measuring Impact and Communicating Success

1. *Data Collection:* What systems do you have in place for collecting data on sales enablement effectiveness?

2. *Communication:* How will you tailor your success stories to different stakeholder groups?

3. *Continuous Improvement:* How will you use the data collected to refine and enhance your sales enablement programs?

Chapter 7: Scaling Sales Enablement Across the Organization

1. *Readiness:* Is your organization prepared for scaling sales enablement programs? What barriers might you face?

2. *Customization:* How will you balance the need for consistency with the need for customization across different teams or regions?

3. *Governance:* What governance structures will you establish to manage the scaling process effectively?

RESOURCES

GLOSSARY OF SALES ENABLEMENT TERMS

Account-Based Selling (ABS): A sales strategy that focuses on targeting specific high-value accounts with personalized campaigns, aiming to build relationships with key stakeholders within those accounts.

ADDIE Model: An instructional design framework that stands for Analyze, Design, Develop, Implement, and Evaluate. It provides a systematic approach to creating effective training programs by guiding designers through each phase of the development process.

Adoption Rate: The percentage of sales reps actively using new tools, processes, or content introduced by the sales enablement team.

Artificial Intelligence (AI): The simulation of human intelligence processes by machines, particularly computer systems, used in sales enablement for predictive analytics, personalized coaching, content generation, and automating tasks.

Blended Learning: An educational approach that combines online digital media with traditional face-to-face methods, providing interactive and self-paced learning experiences.

Buyer's Journey: The process buyers go through to become aware of, evaluate, and decide to purchase a new product or service.

Canva: An online graphic design platform used to create visual content such as presentations, social media graphics, and marketing materials. Its user-friendly interface allows sales and marketing teams to produce professional designs without extensive graphic design experience.

Channeltivity: A partner relationship management (PRM) software that helps organizations manage and optimize their sales channel programs. It provides tools for partner onboarding, deal registration, lead management, and analytics to strengthen channel partnerships.

ChatBlackGPT: An AI language model and platform founded by Erin Reddick designed to address biases in AI outputs and promote culturally inclusive language. It aims to provide more equitable and representative responses by considering diverse perspectives and backgrounds.

Circle.so: A platform for building and managing online communities. Circle.so provides tools for creating customizable community spaces, integrating discussions, content sharing, events, and networking features. It enables organizations to foster engagement, collaboration, and communication among members, enhancing team connectivity and knowledge sharing in sales enablement programs.

Clay: A generative AI tool that automates data collection and enrichment processes. It helps sales teams gather and organize prospect information, enabling more personalized and effective outreach.

Content Management System (CMS): Software that helps create, manage, and modify digital content, often used to organize and distribute sales and marketing materials.

Cross-Selling: The practice of selling an additional product or service to an existing customer, enhancing the value of the original purchase.

Customer Relationship Management (CRM): Technology systems like Salesforce or HubSpot that manage a company's interactions with current and potential customers, using data analysis to improve business relationships.

Customer Success: A function focused on ensuring customers achieve their desired outcomes while using a company's product or service, often leading to increased loyalty and retention.

Data-Driven Strategy: Making decisions and strategies based on data analysis and interpretation rather than intuition.

DeepLearning.AI: An education technology company founded by Andrew Ng that offers specialized courses in artificial intelligence and deep learning. Their programs, available on platforms like Coursera, help professionals develop skills in AI, machine learning, and data science.

EMPOWER Model: A framework for driving engagement and motivation in sales enablement programs. Steps are Engage, Motivate, Provide Resources, Optimize Processes, Win Together, Evaluate, Recognize.

Enablement Content: Materials created to assist sales reps in engaging prospects effectively, including sales scripts, case studies, presentations, and product overviews.

Generative AI Tools: Artificial intelligence applications that can generate content such as text, images, or videos. Examples include Clay, Jasper, and Synthesia.ai.

Instructional Design: The practice of creating educational experiences that make the acquisition of knowledge and skill more efficient, effective, and appealing.

Inclusive Design: Designing training programs that are accessible and usable by as many people as possible, regardless of age, ability, or circumstance.

Instructional Systems Design (ISD): The practice of creating educational and training programs in a consistent and reliable fashion to improve learner performance and retention.

Jasper: An AI-powered writing assistant that generates human-like text for various purposes, including marketing copy, emails, social media posts, and more. It aids sales and marketing teams in creating content efficiently.

Jordan Godbey: A consultant specializing in building and growing online communities, particularly using platforms like Circle.so. Jordan assists organizations in leveraging online communities to enhance engagement, foster collaboration, and support sales enablement initiatives. He can be reached at jordan@growth-community.co for consultations and support.

Key Performance Indicators (KPIs): Quantifiable measures used to evaluate the success of an organization, employee, or process in meeting objectives for performance.

Learning Management System (LMS): Software applications for the administration, documentation, tracking, reporting, automation, and delivery of educational courses or training programs. Examples include Thinkific and Coursera.

Learning Styles: The preferred ways in which individuals learn. Common styles include visual, auditory, kinesthetic, and reading/writing.

Microlearning: An educational approach that delivers content in small, specific bursts, allowing learners to control what and when they're learning.

Multimedia Learning Principles: Guidelines for using words and pictures to enhance learning, such as the use of relevant visuals, avoiding extraneous content, and aligning narration with imagery.

Neuroscience in Learning: Applying findings from neuroscience to enhance training effectiveness, such as spacing learning over time, using storytelling, and engaging emotions.

Online Communities: Virtual spaces where individuals or organizations interact, share information, and build relationships around shared interests or goals. In sales enablement, online communities facilitate knowledge sharing, peer support, collaboration, and continuous learning among sales teams.

Onboarding: The process of integrating a new employee into an organization, providing them with the necessary knowledge, skills, and behaviors to become effective members of the team.

Peer Coaching: A collaborative learning method where sales representatives support each other's development through sharing knowledge, providing feedback, and practicing skills together. Peer coaching involves activities such as role-playing sales scenarios, discussing challenges, and offering constructive critiques.

Pipeline Management: The process of overseeing and directing future sales in various stages of the sales process, ensuring steady revenue growth.

Predictive Analytics: The use of data, statistical algorithms, and machine learning techniques to identify the likelihood of future outcomes based on historical data.

Professor Jules White: A faculty member at Vanderbilt University and an expert in computer science and engineering. He offers courses on generative AI and prompt engineering on platforms like Coursera, providing valuable insights into the application of AI in various fields, including sales enablement.

Role-Playing Exercises: Training activities where participants act out scenarios to practice skills and behaviors in a simulated environment.

SAM Model (Successive Approximation Model): An agile instructional design model that emphasizes iterative development and collaboration. Unlike linear models, SAM allows for rapid prototyping and continuous feedback throughout the design process.

SAM I: Focuses on small projects with quick iterations.

SAM II: Suited for larger projects, incorporating more extensive planning and development phases.

Sales Coaching: A developmental process where sales managers provide guidance, feedback, and support to sales reps to improve their performance and achieve sales goals.

Sales Cycle: The series of predictable phases required to sell a product or service, from initial contact to closing the deal.

Sales Enablement: A strategic, ongoing process that equips all client-facing employees with the ability to consistently have valuable conversations with the right set of customer stakeholders at each stage of the customer's problem-solving life cycle.

Sales Enablement Instructional Design (SEID): A framework for creating effective sales training programs, emphasizing four key components: Specific, Engaging, Interactive, and Design.

Sales Engagement Platform: Technology that helps sales teams manage, track, and optimize interactions with prospects and customers across multiple touchpoints.

Sales Funnel: A model that represents the stages a customer goes through in the sales process, from awareness to purchase, often visualized as a funnel due to the decreasing number of prospects at each stage.

Sales Methodology: A set of guiding principles and practices that define how your sales process should be carried out to increase efficiency and effectiveness.

Sales Playbook: A document that outlines your company's sales strategies, tactics, best practices, and resources, serving as a guide for sales reps.

Sales Process: A systematic sequence of steps that a salesperson follows to guide a prospect from initial contact to purchase.

SCALE Framework: A strategy for scaling sales enablement programs across an organization. Follows the steps Standardize, Customize, Align, Leverage Technology, and Evaluate and Iterate.

SEAL Framework: A methodology for creating impactful training by ensuring it is Strategic, Engaging, Actionable, and Legit.

Social Learning Theory: The concept that people learn from one another through observation, imitation, and modeling, emphasizing the importance of social interactions in learning.

Synthesia.ai: An AI video creation platform that allows users to produce professional-quality videos with digital avatars and voiceovers without the need for cameras or studios. It's used for creating training videos, product demos, and personalized messages at scale.

Thinkific: An online course platform that enables individuals and businesses to create, market, and sell their own customized courses. It's used for training programs, continuing education, and professional development.

Time-to-Productivity: The time it takes for a new sales rep to reach full productivity and contribute meaningfully to the company's revenue.

Universal Design for Learning (UDL): A framework for optimizing teaching and learning by providing multiple means of representation, engagement, and expression to accommodate individual learning differences.

Upselling: The practice of encouraging customers to purchase a higher-end product or add-on services to increase the value of the sale.

Virtual Reality (VR) and Augmented Reality (AR): Technologies that create immersive experiences. VR provides a completely virtual environment, while AR overlays virtual elements onto the real-world. In sales enablement, they are used for simulations, product demonstrations, and interactive training experiences.

Web Content Accessibility Guidelines (WCAG): A set of guidelines developed by the World Wide Web Consortium (W3C) to make web content more accessible to people with disabilities. Compliance ensures that training materials are usable by all members of the sales team.

SUMMARY OF RECOMMENDED TECH STACK TOOLS

By assembling a well-rounded tech stack from the categories above, organizations can enhance their sales enablement efforts, streamline operations, and ensure teams have the right tools to succeed. Also note: This is a continually changing list, companies merge, and Generative AI is continually adding functionality to platforms enhancing their value.

Here is a summary of the recommended tools categorized by their function:

Customer Relationship Management (CRM) Systems

- **HubSpot CRM:** A user-friendly CRM with built-in marketing automation, ideal for aligning sales and marketing efforts.

- **Microsoft Dynamics 365:** Integrates seamlessly with other Microsoft products, offering comprehensive CRM and ERP solutions.

- **Pipedrive:** Provides intuitive and visual pipeline management, mobile-friendly, focusing on driving deals to completion.

- **Salesforce:** A leading CRM platform offering extensive customization, integration capabilities, and a robust ecosystem of add-ons.

- **Zoho CRM:** Affordable, with a wide range of features including AI-driven insights from Zia. Strong automation capabilities.

Learning Management Systems (LMS)

- **Absorb LMS:** Great for enterprises and training companies. Excellent UI, filtering, and scalability for internal/external training.

- **Allego:** Offers mobile-friendly, on-demand learning and video coaching tools.

- **Canvas LMS:** Suitable for academic and corporate training, with detailed analytics and extensive integrations.

- **Channeltivity:** Ideal for partner and channel programs, providing scalable training options.

- **Docebo:** Highly configurable and future-focused with AI integrations, ideal for fast-growing international companies.

- **Lessonly:** Focused on ease of use, enabling quick creation and delivery of training content.

- **Mindtickle:** Provides gamification, personalized learning paths, and AI-driven coaching features.

- **Thinkific:** A user-friendly solution for smaller-scale learning needs.

Sales Enablement Platforms

- **Circle.so:** Customizable online community platform for accessible, searchable content, events, and learning resources.

- **GetGuru:** Offers just-in-time content presentation, making all your content easily searchable and accessible.

- **Highspot:** AI-powered search, content management, and analytics platform to improve sales effectiveness.

- **Seismic:** Personalized content delivery, sales analytics, and CRM integration for streamlined enablement efforts.

- **Showpad:** Combines content management with interactive sales tools and training capabilities.

- **Spekit:** Embeds just-in-time learning and AI-powered knowledge into workflows, plus customizable playbooks.

- **Ultraluminal:** A cutting-edge platform leveraging AI to streamline and accelerate the sales enablement process.

Sales Engagement Platforms

- **AI-Supported Platforms:** An emerging category of generative AI tools integrating with existing solutions or as stand-alone applications.

- **Mixmax:** Enhances email communication with tracking, scheduling, and automation features.

- **Outreach:** Automates multi-channel communication sequences and provides analytics.

- **Salesloft:** Offers sales cadence automation, call analytics, and CRM integration to streamline sales outreach.

Content Management Systems (CMS)

(Note: Some sales enablement platforms include CMS functionality.)

- Highspot (also listed under Sales Enablement Platforms)

- **Microsoft 365:** Tools can be leveraged for document storage, sharing, and management.

- Seismic (also listed under Sales Enablement Platforms)

Analytics and Business Intelligence Tools

- **Clari:** Specializes in sales forecasting, pipeline management, and provides AI-driven insights.

- **Microsoft Power BI:** Integrates with Microsoft products for robust business analytics and intelligence.

- **Tableau:** Offers data visualization and interactive dashboards to analyze sales performance and trends.

Collaboration and Communication Tools

- **Asana:** Project and task management, promoting cross-team transparency and collaboration.

- **Microsoft Teams:** Integrated chat, meeting, and file collaboration within the Office 365 suite.

- **Slack:** Channel-based team communication, direct messaging, and extensive integration capabilities.

Online Community Platforms

- **Circle.so:** Build online communities for peer-to-peer interaction, knowledge sharing, and engagement among sales teams and customers.

Sales Coaching and Conversation Intelligence Tools

- **Chorus.ai:** Analyzes sales interactions to provide coaching opportunities and actionable feedback.

- **Gong:** Uses AI to analyze calls and meetings, offering insights to refine sales conversations and strategies.

Marketing Automation Tools

- **Marketo:** Automates marketing tasks, nurtures leads, and aligns efforts with sales strategies.

- **Pardot:** Salesforce's B2B marketing automation solution, closely integrated with Salesforce CRM.

Customer Success Platforms

- **Gainsight:** Manages customer relationships, monitors health scores, and improves retention.

- **Totango:** Drives customer success initiatives, tracks engagement, and increases product adoption.

Additional Tools

- **Calendly:** Simplifies meeting scheduling with integration to calendars and automated reminders.

- **Zoom:** Facilitates video conferencing and virtual meetings for remote sales engagements and training.

FURTHER READING AND RESOURCE LIST

To continue your learning journey and deepen your understanding of sales enablement, consider exploring the following books, articles, and resources. This curated selection is designed to be comprehensive yet not overwhelming, guiding you toward reliable, actionable insights. Consider exploring a few key resources first, then expanding as your needs and interests evolve.

Books

Agile Selling: Get Up to Speed Quickly in Today's Ever-Changing Sales World by Jill Konrath

Why Read: Offers practical strategies to rapidly learn and adapt, a must in dynamic markets.

Cracking the Sales Management Code: The Secrets to Measuring and Managing Sales Performance by Jason Jordan and Michelle Vazzana

Why Read: Focuses on metrics and processes that drive tangible sales outcomes, helping leaders measure what matters.

Sales Enablement: A Master Framework to Engage, Equip, and Empower a World-Class Sales Force by Byron Matthews and Tamara Schenk

Why Read: Provides a comprehensive, strategic framework for implementing and evolving sales enablement programs.

The Challenger Sale: Taking Control of the Customer Conversation by Matthew Dixon and Brent Adamson

Why Read: Reinvents the sales conversation approach, emphasizing teaching, tailoring, and taking control to differentiate your offering.

The Sales Enablement Playbook by Cory Bray and Hilmon Sorey

Why Read: Offers clear, actionable steps to implement and refine your sales enablement strategy at any stage.

Articles and Reports

Sales Enablement Analytics: The Essentials by Forrester Research

Why Read: Understand how analytics drive better decision-making and prove ROI in your enablement efforts.

State of Sales Enablement by Sales Enablement PRO

Why Read: Annual industry insights and trends to keep you current and benchmark your program's progress.

The Ultimate Guide to Sales Enablement by HubSpot

Why Read: A comprehensive online guide covering core concepts, strategies, and tools, great for a quick foundational refresher.

Websites and Online Communities

Community.Jasper.ai Community on Circle.so

Why Visit: Connect with peers interested in generative AI and sales enablement, expanding your network and knowledge. View an example of a well designed online community.

Modern Sales Pros

Why Visit: Engage with a community of sales operations and enablement leaders, ask questions, and share best practices.

Sales Enablement Society (SES)

Why Visit: A professional association dedicated to advancing sales enablement; find events, discussions, and thought leadership.

Saleshood

Why Visit: Offers resources, training, and community discussions focused on driving sales productivity and performance.

Online Courses and Certifications

Certified Sales Enablement Professional (CSEP) by ATD

Why Take It: A recognized credential that validates your expertise and commitment to sales enablement best practices.

Sales Enablement Certificate Program by LinkedIn Learning

Why Take It: A structured learning path to build or refine your enablement skills, featuring industry experts.

Sales Enablement Certification by HubSpot Academy

Why Take It: Free, foundational course that covers core enablement principles and practical implementation tips.

Blogs and Thought Leaders

Mike Kunkle's Transforming Sales Results

Why Read: Insights from a seasoned practitioner on improving sales performance and enablement initiatives.

Sales Enablement Collective Blog

Why Read: Regular updates, interviews, and insights from a variety of enablement professionals across industries.

Tamara Schenk's Blog

Why Read: In-depth thought leadership from a recognized expert, focusing on strategy, process, and data-driven enablement.

NOTE: The availability and relevance of these resources as content and access may change over time.

Top Podcasts on Sales Enablement

Engaging with industry podcasts is an excellent way to stay informed about the latest trends, strategies, and insights in sales enablement. Here are five top podcasts that provide valuable content for sales enablement professionals:

Sales Enablement PRO Podcast

Why Listen: Interviews with industry leaders tackling re-al-world challenges, trends, and best practices in enablement.

Sales Hacker Podcast

Why Listen: Stays at the forefront of sales trends, discussing practical strategies and emerging technologies.

Stats on Stats Podcast

Why Listen: Explores trends in tech and cybersecurity, offering insights that can inform and protect your sales strategy.

The Audible-Ready Podcast

Why Listen: Topics range from messaging to buyer engagement, helping align sales strategies with customer needs.

The Sales Enablement Podcast with Andy Paul

Why Listen: Features diverse thought leaders sharing actionable advice to improve sales performance and productivity.

> **NOTE:** Podcast availability and content may change over time. It's recommended to check for the latest episodes and sub-scribe through your preferred podcast platform.

BUILD A KICKA$$ SALES TEAM

ACKNOWLEDGMENTS

I am deeply grateful to the colleagues, mentors, and teams who have helped shape my understanding of sales enablement over the years. Your guidance, thought-provoking questions, and willingness to push boundaries have influenced every page of this book. To the countless sales professionals working tirelessly to elevate their craft: Your dedication, ingenuity, and resilience have been a constant source of inspiration.

A heartfelt thank you to my spouse, Trish N. Kedar, for your unwavering support, patience, and encouragement throughout this journey. Your steadfast belief in my vision, and your ability to keep me grounded, have been instrumental in bringing this work to fruition. Your love and understanding have given me the confidence and clarity to share these insights with the world.

ABOUT THE AUTHOR

DR. EVE KEDAR

Dr. Eve Kedar is a respected sales enablement expert known for designing and implementing impactful training, certification, and community-building programs that enhance revenue growth. Her influence spans global tech leaders like Apple, Seagate, and Gainsight, as well as agile startup environments, where her strategic guidance consistently drives measurable performance improvements.

PROFESSIONAL HIGHLIGHTS

- **Transformational Sales Enablement:** At Seagate, Dr. Kedar led the Systems Selling Academy, achieving 80%+ completion rates and contributing to a 20% increase in sales growth. She also developed the Ensighten Academy—featuring three comprehensive certification paths and a 100+ video self-enablement library—empowering Fortune 500 clients to achieve lasting, scalable results.

- **Thought Leadership:** Recognized by MindTouch as a Top 100 Customer Success Influencer and profiled by the Sales Enablement Society (SES) in their "Faces of Sales Enablement" series, Dr. Kedar's insights span best practices, forward-thinking strategies, and community engagement that enrich the broader sales enablement ecosystem.

- **Innovator in Generative AI:** Pioneering the integration of generative AI tools into training workflows, Dr. Kedar enhances learning experiences, ensures they address output bias and accelerates team readiness, ensuring organizations remain agile and competitive in rapidly evolving markets.

ACADEMIC CREDENTIALS

- **Doctorate in Education and Leadership for Change, Fielding Graduate University, Santa Barbara:** Dr. Kedar's academic foundation informs her evidence-based, learner-centric approach, ensuring that her enablement programs are both innovative and grounded in proven educational frameworks.

PERSONAL NOTE

Beyond the professional sphere, Dr. Kedar lives with her wife and their two dogs, Ollie and Mowglie, and volunteers as a guide at the Monterey Bay Aquarium—a reflection of her lifelong passion for exploration, education, and community. Her articles and insights can be found at evekedar.ghost.io, and you can learn more about her consulting services at EKConsulting.io. To connect directly, visit her LinkedIn profile: linkedin.com/in/evekedar/.

Whether helping sales teams embrace new strategies, adopt cutting-edge technologies, or foster thriving learning communities, Dr. Eve Kedar is dedicated to empowering organizations to achieve their boldest sales enablement ambitions.